**designing
systems
programs**

Prentice-Hall
Series in Automatic Computation
George Forsythe, editor

ARBIB, *Theories of Abstract Automata*
BATES AND DOUGLAS, *Programming Language/One*
BAUMANN, FELICIANO, BAUER, AND SAMELSON, *Introduction to ALGOL*
BLUMENTHAL, *Management Information Systems*
BOBROW AND SCHWARTZ, EDITORS, *Computers and the Policy-Making Community:
    Applications to International Relations*
BOWLES, EDITOR, *Computers in Humanistic Research*
CRESS, DIRKSEN, AND GRAHAM, *FORTRAN IV with Whatfor*
DANIEL, *Theory and Methods for the Approximate Minimization of Functionals*
DESMONDE, *Computers and Their Uses*
EVANS, WALLACE, AND SUTHERLAND, *Simulation Using Digital Computers*
FIKE, *Computer Evaluation of Mathematical Functions*
FIKE, *PL/1 for Scientific Programmers*
FORSYTHE AND MOLER, *Computer Solution of Linear Algebraic Systems*
GAUTHIER AND PONTO, *Designing Systems Programs*
GOLDEN, *FORTRAN IV: Programming and Computing*
GOLDEN AND LEICHUS, *IBM 360: Programming and Computing*
GORDON, *System Simulation*
GREENSPAN, *Lectures on the Numerical Solution of Linear, Singular and Nonlinear Differential
    Equations*
GRISWOLD, POAGE, AND POLONSKY, *The SNOBOL4 Programming Language*
HARTMANIS AND STEARNS, *Algebraic Structure Theory of Sequential Machines*
HULL, *Introduction to Computing*
HUSSON, *Microprogramming: Principles and Practices*
JOHNSON, *System Structure in Data, Programs, and Computers*
KIVIAT, VILLANUEVA, AND MARKOWITZ, *The SIMSCRIPT II Programming Language*
LOUDEN, *Programming the IBM 1130 and 1180*
MARTIN, *Design of Real-Time Computer Systems*
MARTIN, *Programming Real-Time Computer Systems*
MARTIN, *Telecommunications and the Computer*
MARTIN, *Teleprocessing Network Organization*
MARTIN AND NORMAN, *The Computerized Society*
MATHISON AND WALKER, *Computers and Telecommunications: Issue in Public Policy*
MCKEEMAN et al., *A Compiler Generator*
MINSKY, *Computation: Finite and Infinite Machines*
MOORE, *Interval Analysis*
PYLYSHYN, *Perspectives on the Computer Revolution*
PRITSKER AND KIVIAT, *Simulation with GASP II: A FORTRAN Based Simulation Language*
SAMMET, *Programming Languages: History and Fundamentals*
STERLING AND POLLACK, *Introduction to Statistical Data Processing*
TAVISS, *The Computer Impact*
TRAUB, *Iterative Methods for the Solution of Equations*
VARGA, *Matrix Iterative Analysis*
VAZSONYI, *Problem Solving by Digital Computers with PL/1 Programming*
WILKINSON, *Rounding Errors in Algebraic Processes*

Designing Systems Programs

Richard L. Gauthier
R.L.G. Associates, Inc.

Stephen D. Ponto
System Industries, Inc.

Prentice-Hall, Inc., Englewood Cliffs, New Jersey

Current printing (last digit): 10 9 8 7 6 5 4 3 2

13-201962-0

Library of Congress Catalog Card Number 74-101201

Printed in the United States of America

PRENTICE-HALL INTERNATIONAL, INC., *London*
PRENTICE-HALL OF AUSTRALIA, PTY. LTD., *Sydney*
PRENTICE-HALL OF CANADA, LTD., *Toronto*
PRENTICE-HALL OF INDIA PRIVATE LTD., *New Delhi*
PRENTICE-HALL OF JAPAN, INC., *Tokyo*

Dedicated to our families:
Patricia and Darrin Gauthier
Nancy, Chris, and Betsy Ponto

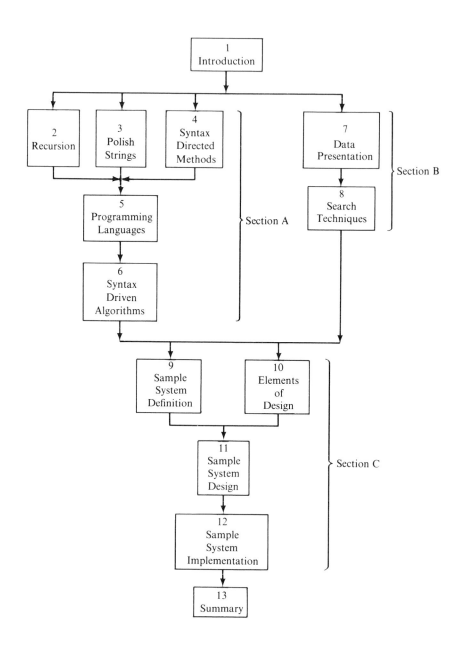

Dependence diagram

preface

This book is written for the technically oriented person who has programmed a digital computer. As a text the book provides an introduction to systems programming for students versed in machine language or compiler programming. As a reference the book serves as a collection of programming techniques currently used in the field.

Subject matter

The book approaches critical areas of systems design and implementation from a technical viewpoint. System techniques are discussed in terms of design logic, application criterion, and implementation methodology.

Wherever applicable, techniques are illustrated by flow charts and schematic diagrams so that the reader may transfer them directly to the computer.

Organization

The book is organized so that each chapter calls on only those concepts and techniques discussed in previous chapters. Chapters are grouped into three sections. Sections A and B present basic techniques in logic management and data management, respectively. Section C presents applications which draw on these techniques.

While the book is written for a cover-to-cover reading of all material, the reader may choose to read only selected topics. The dependence diagram on page vi is intended as a guide for such a reader. This diagram presents the logical dependence of chapters within the book.

Terminology and presentation

We have tried to keep the terminology in this book as simple as possible in order to relieve you, the reader, from mastering an unnecessarily extended set of unfamiliar terms. When new terms are used they are defined as they are introduced; since most of these terms are well defined in the programming field, our definition is likely to be a reinforcement of your knowledge.

Some of the programming techniques are sufficiently complex to warrant coding specification. For such presentation we have used schematic diagrams, flow charts, and FORTRAN-like programming statements. We have not used machine language. It is our belief that you will find this presentation quite readable and easy to understand, and that you will also find the techniques readily translatable to the computer.

Acknowledgments

We are grateful to the many individuals who made constructive suggestions in the course of text preparation. In particular, we wish to thank Dave Ferguson for his assistance on the balanced tree search/insert/delete methods and Howard Medcalf for the knowledge gained from his article on syntax directed methods.

Richard L. Gauthier
Stephen D. Ponto

contents

1
introduction

A computer programming system is designed to respond under direction of programmed command. The system itself is only a collection of algorithms and computational procedures for the performance of generalized computing tasks. To operate on a specific task the system must be directed. It then applies its algorithms and procedures to the requested task as directed by programmed command. Of special interest is the case in which commands are given by a human being. In such a system the command structure is supported by a command language; of primary importance to the system is the processing of this language.

This book presents basic concepts and techniques for systems language processing. Among these are some fairly powerful techniques for automatic acceptance and breakdown of a free-form language. The presentation begins with basics in systems programming and builds in scope to the design and development of complete systems. To illustrate technique construction, text description is supplemented by schematic diagrams, flow charts, compiler-like coding, and trace tables. The reader will readily be able to translate these illustrations to machine language for the computer of his choice.

As a framework for computing techniques we will take a brief look at the system design process. Designers must first have been implementors; they must be knowledgeable in the limitations and restrictions of available computing techniques in order to create a correct or optimum design. For this reason we will not go into great detail over design until the last section of the book. When looking at computing techniques, however, it is well to have a basic grasp of the design process.

The design of language processing systems is conceptually no different from the design of other programming systems. Each declares a plan for system development. In that plan the system is divided into composite modules: logic modules for processing operations of the system and data modules for the system data base. This division is, in itself, a plan for the system. It permits independent development of each of the system modules.

This book is divided into three sections. The first presents techniques in logic, the second techniques in data management. The final section applies these techniques to the design and development of language processing systems. Together the three sections provide a complete and integrated approach to the topic of computerized language processing.

A.

techniques in logic

In the basic design a language processing application is segmented into small modules, and the purpose and function of each module is precisely defined. The immediate question encountered is how the purpose and function of each module can be effected; that is to say, what techniques are available for implementing the modules. It is only natural to begin with techniques for the logic modules. The logic modules provide the flow and pattern of the system. Examination of techniques for these modules provides further insight and clarification to the entire structure.

This section presents techniques for writing logic modules—the processing modules of the language processing application. These techniques are

not difficult to grasp. By a careful reading the reader with limited programming experience can extend his understanding of systems methods. By
skimming these techniques the systems programmer or analyst can reinforce
his own methods and procedures for program construction.

2
recursion

One of the basic techniques useful for language processing is recursion. Recursion can simplify the analysis and acceptance of arithmetic or Boolean expressions; as the book progresses we will see further uses for recursive processes.

An example of recursion is available in elementary mathematics. We may define the factorial function [factorial$(n) = n * (n - 1) * (n - 2) * \cdots * (3) * (2) * (1)$] in recursive form as follows.

$$\text{factorial}\,(n) = \begin{cases} 1 \text{ if } n = 1 \\ n * \text{factorial}\,(n - 1) \text{ if } n > 1 \end{cases}$$

Hence factorial(3) = 3 * factorial(2) = 3 * 2 * factorial(1) = 3 * 2 * 1.

The above is only a definition of the factorial function, not a procedure for computing the functional value. In a computing environment we could formulate such a procedure. Based on the above definition, this procedure will accept a parameter (N). Call this parameter the recursion parameter. At each iteration the procedure will call itself with an updated recursion parameter value.

```
RECURSIVE PROCEDURE FACTORIAL (N)
IF N > 1 THEN ANSWER = N * FACTORIAL (N − 1)
    ELSE ANSWER = 1
END
```

2.1. Parameter Tracking

There are special requirements in a recursive procedure to keep track of where and how the procedure is called. First, the procedure must return to the proper location when processing is finished. Since the procedure may be called from several places within or outside itself, it has to keep track of where it was called so that it may return to the proper location at completion. Secondly, the procedure must keep track of how the parameters were specified for each call. These parameters define how the procedure is called and, consequently, how the procedure must release control at completion. To perform this tracking the procedure must save parameters upon entry and restore these parameters at completion.

2.2. Algorithm Structure

Saving and restoring parameters for tracking imposes a consistent structure on a recursive procedure. The body of the procedure is visually preceded by a prologue to save parameters and followed by an epilogue to restore parameters. An example of a recursive procedure with two calls to itself and minor internal processing might be flow charted as shown in Fig. 2.1.

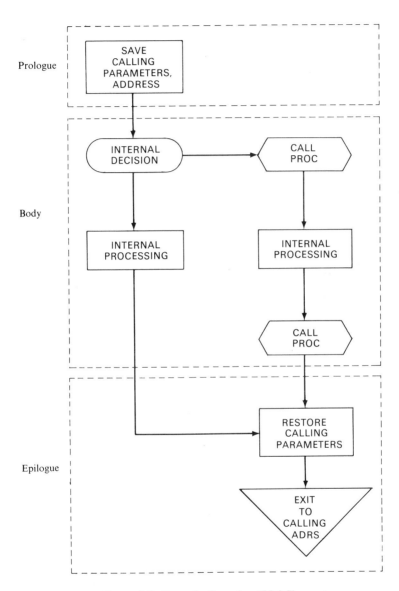

Figure 2.1. Recursive Procedure 'PROC'.

2.3. Tracking Order

Parameters must be tracked in a specific order. *The last parameters saved are the first parameters to be restored.* The first exit from the procedure is to the point of last invocation. This tracking order will become evident very shortly when we examine examples of recursive procedures. This last saved–first restored order will have to be taken temporarily on faith while we examine the save and restore mechanism in detail.

2.4. Stack Memory

A stack table is normally used for tracking parameters in a recursive procedure. Logically the stack functions as a last in–first out storage mechanism. Whenever an item is taken from the stack it is the last item that had been inserted. Physically the stack constitutes a simple form of data table. There is a pointer at the front of the table designating the current end of stack, as shown in Fig. 2.2.

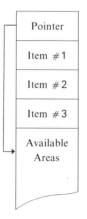

Figure 2.2. Stack table.

When an item is stacked it is physically moved to the area designated by the pointer; the pointer is incremented to reflect the insertion. To remove an item the pointer is decremented and the last item moved out. Figures 2.3 and 2.4 serve as examples of this.

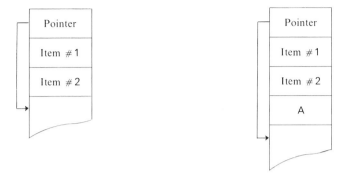

Figure 2.3. STACK A operation.

Figure 2.4. UNSTACK A operation.

2.5. Algorithm Examples

2.5.1. Factorial Example

The factorial example may be written recursively in compiler language as follows.

```
RECURSIVE PROCEDURE FACTORIAL (N)
IF N > 1 THEN ANSWER = N * FACTORIAL (N − 1)
     ELSE ANSWER = 1
END
```

Let us look at the underlying computer operations supporting this procedure. They are flow charted as shown in Fig. 2.5. In tracing this procedure

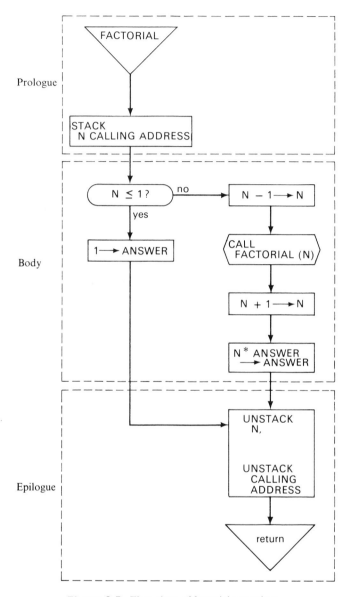

Figure 2.5. Flow chart of factorial procedure.

we can see the operation of the last in–first out stack. A step-by-step trace of
the procedure following an initial call CALL FACTORIAL(3) appears as

$$N = 3$$

First iteration

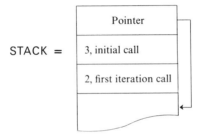

$$N = 2$$
CALL FACTORIAL(2)

Second iteration

STACK =

Pointer
3, initial call
2, first iteration call

$$N = 1$$
CALL FACTORIAL(1)

Third iteration

STACK =

Pointer
3, initial call
2, first iteration call
1, second iteration call

ANSWER = 1

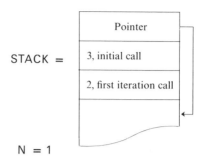

STACK =

Pointer
3, initial call
2, first iteration call

N = 1

Return to second iteration

N = 2

ANSWER = 2 * 1

STACK =

Pointer
3, initial call

N = 2

Return to first iteration

N = 3

ANSWER = 3 * 2 * 1

STACK = empty =

Pointer

N = 3

Return to initial call.

As can be seen, the correct value for factorial 3 was computed and saved in ANSWER.

2.5.2. Permutation Example

A more interesting application for recursion is the problem of listing all permutations of a character string. For instance, all 24 orderings for the four character string ABCD are

ABCD	BACD	CABD	DABC
ABDC	BADC	CADB	DACB
ACBD	BDAC	CBAD	DBAC
ACDB	BDCA	CBDA	DBCA
ADBC	BCAD	CDAB	DCAB
ADCB	BCDA	CDBA	DCBA

A recursive procedure can be written to solve the general case of permuting an N character string as follows.

```
RECURSIVE PROCEDURE PERMUTE(STRING,N)
    DO I = 1 TO N
    IF N = 2
        DO
        PUT(STRING)
        CALL ROTATE(STRING,N)
        END
    ELSE
        DO
        CALL PERMUTE(STRING,N − 1)
        CALL ROTATE(STRING,N)
        END
    END ORDER
```

The auxiliary procedure ROTATE (STRING,N) rotates the first N characters of STRING by one position. For example, ROTATE ('ABCDEFG',5) rotates the first five characters ABCDE one position to BCDEA producing the resulting string BCDEAFG.

```
PROCEDURE ROTATE(STRING,N)
    SAVE = STRING(1)
    DO I = 1 TO N − 1 STRING(I) = STRING(I + 1)
    STRING(N) = SAVE
    END
```

For a more detailed description of the recursive procedure let us look at a flow chart of PERMUTE (Fig. 2.6). As demonstrated in this flow chart, not only formal recursion parameters require tracking, but also all working variables internal to the recursive procedure. In this case the working variable "I" must be tracked.

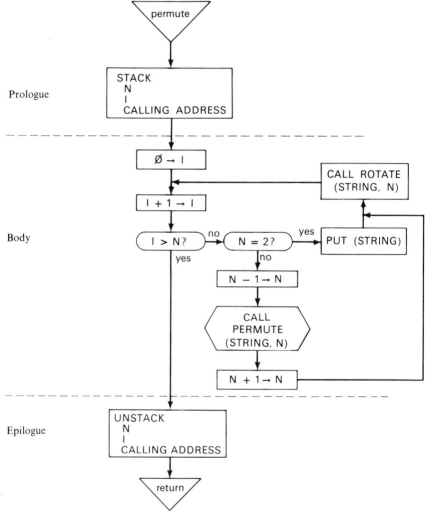

Figure 2.6. Flow chart of permute procedure.

Again we will trace the procedure. Let us start with a permutation of the three character string ABC. Initial call CALL PERMUTE('ABC',3) appears as

$$N = 3$$
$$STRING = ABC$$

First iteration

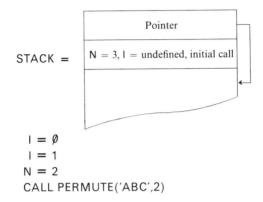

STACK =

Pointer

N = 3, I = undefined, initial call

I = ∅
I = 1
N = 2
CALL PERMUTE('ABC',2)

Second iteration

STACK =

Pointer

N = 3, I = undefined, initial call

N = 2, I = 1   , first iteration call

I = ∅
I = 1
PUT 'ABC'
CALL ROTATE(STRING,2)
STRING = 'BAC'
I = 2
PUT 'BAC'
CALL ROTATE(STRING,2)
STRING = 'ABC'
I = 3

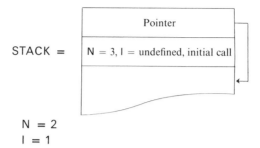

$$N = 2$$
$$I = 1$$

return to first iteration

$$N = 3$$
CALL ROTATE (STRING,3)
STRING = 'BCA'
$$I = 2$$
$$N = 2$$
CALL PERMUTE ('BCA',2)

Third iteration

etc.

Two further examples of recursion are the syntax driver and the Polish synthesis algorithm covered in later sections of the book.

2.6. Summary

The stack table is basic to the recursion process. A recursive procedure may roughly be defined as a procedure that calls itself. In calling itself it must keep track of the recursion parameters. Parameters are kept in a stack table. Upon entry to the procedure the parameters are saved; upon exit they are restored. The stack table supports a last in–first out save–restore order. This is the proper order for parameter tracking.

2.7
exercises

(1) Form your own definition of a recursive procedure.

(2) Does parameter tracking impose a consistent structure on a recursive procedure?

(3) Why are parameters tracked in a recursive procedure?

(4) What mechanism can be used to save the tracked parameters? Show a schematic diagram of the mechanism.

(5) In what order are parameters tracked?

3
polish strings

In this day and age of algebraic compilers and information management systems there is an increasing need to process Boolean and arithmetic expressions. Engineers, scientists, and business executives wish to communicate with the computer in their own language environment. For example, a corporate manpower search might be conducted through a conversational information management system with the query: IF DEGREE = BA|BS & PROFESSION = ENGINEER| (AGE > 35 & EXPERIENCE = SUPERVISOR) LIST NAME. An engineering reading might be effected on a desk calculator with the command: PRINT SQRT[[(X_1 − X_2) ↑ 2 + (Y_1 − Y_2) ↑ 2]/2]. In either case the supporting computer program must process an expression. The expression is written in standard text copy form.

3.1. Standard Expression Form

The standard form of expression presentation permits complicated priority structures based on parenthetical groupings. These structures are resolved naturally by human beings. Through experience and learning we know that the value of the expression $6 - 4 + 7 = 9$ is the same as the value for $(6 - 4) + 7 = 9$ but different from the value for $6 - (4 + 7) = -5$. We know this because we can naturally apply the following rules.

(1) Operators normally apply to two operands: the operand preceding and the operand following the operator.
(2) Operators are normally (but not always) evaluated in a left-to-right order.
(3) Parentheses override the normal order of evaluation.

These rules permit us to analyze the three expressions as follows.

$$
\begin{array}{ccc}
\underbrace{6 - 4}_{2} + 7 & \underbrace{(6 - 4)}_{2} + 7 & 6 - \underbrace{(4 + 7)}_{11} \\
\underbrace{}_{9} & \underbrace{}_{9} & \underbrace{}_{-5}
\end{array}
$$

The above three rules permit us to evaluate expressions formed with "+" and "−" operators. These rules, however, do not cover all arithmetic expressions. A simple example of this is the expression -4. Leading plus and minus operators (unary plus and unary minus) are not covered in rule 1. These operators apply to only one operand.

A second counter example to our three rules is $6 - 4 * 7$. If we use rule 2 in evaluating this expression we have the erroneous result

$$
\begin{array}{c}
\underbrace{6 - 4}_{2} * 7 \\
\underbrace{}_{14}
\end{array}
$$

Operators are not always evaluated in a left-to-right order. In fact, each operator carries its own priority for order of evaluation. Here multiplication (*) is of higher priority than subtraction ($-$). The priorities for all arithmetic operators generally are

Priority	Operator
1	Unary plus ($+$), Unary minus ($-$)
2	Exponentiation ($\uparrow$)
3	Multiplication (*), Division (/)
4	Addition ($+$), Subtraction ($-$)

Let us now formulate a set of rules to evaluate any arithmetic expression in standard form. These rules are as follows.

(1) Operators normally apply to two operands: the operand preceding and the operand following the operator. Exceptions to this are unary plus and unary minus, which apply to the single operand following the operator.

(2) Operators are evaluated in the order imposed by the following priority structure.

Priority	Operator
1	Unary plus ($+$), Unary minus ($-$)
2	Exponentiation ($\uparrow$)
3	Multiplication (*), Division (/)
4	Addition ($+$), Subtraction ($-$)

Operators of the same priority are evaluated in a left-to-right order.
(3) Parentheses override the normal order of evaluation. Operators inside a pair of parentheses are evaluated first.

With these rules in mind we can evaluate the simple expression $7 * (6 - 4 + 1) \uparrow 2$. By rule 3 we see that "$-$" and "$+$" are enclosed in parentheses and therefore evaluated first. According to rule 2 operators of equal priority are evaluated in left-to-right order. Therefore, of the "$-$" and "$+$" operators, "$-$" is evaluated first. Of the remaining "*" and "$\uparrow$" operators, priorities dictate that "$\uparrow$" will be evaluated first. Therefore the order of operator evaluation is "$-, +, \uparrow, *$" as follows.

$$7 * \underbrace{(6 - 4 + 1)} \uparrow 2$$

$$7 * \underbrace{(2 + 1)} \uparrow 2$$

$$7 * \quad \underbrace{3 \uparrow 2}$$

$$\underbrace{7 * \qquad 9}$$

$$63$$

As stated before, application of these rules comes naturally to a person; they are a product of applied experience with arithmetic expressions. But let us consider how a computer program would have to apply the rules. It would scan the expression for the innermost pair of parentheses, logically sort the included operators on priority, and apply those operators in that order. The program would then have to scan for the next set of parentheses and apply the same process. With all parenthetical subexpressions thus evaluated, the remaining operators would be logically sorted and applied, resulting in a final value for the expression. Three things may be said for this method of expression evaluation: it is slow, it is awkward, and it is difficult to implement.

3.2. Polish Form

Polish strings provide an alternate computing method for processing expressions. Rather than processing the expression in its standard input form, the expression is first broken into a Polish form[1] for internal application. When evaluating an expression that has been translated into Polish form, there are no problems of parenthetical structure or operator priority. In fact there are only two simple rules to apply.

(1) Operators apply to the two operands preceding the operator.
(2) Operators are evaluated in left-to-right order.

---

[1] In this book only post fix Polish forms structured over binary operators will be considered.

The following example illustrates how these rules are applied in evaluating a Polish string.

$$\text{Polish string} \underbrace{4 \quad \underbrace{3 \quad + \quad}_{7} 2 \quad *}$$

$$\underbrace{\qquad\qquad}$$

Value   14

With these two rules in mind we can look at Polish string equivalents for standard form expressions.

In the following examples, simple expressions formed from equal priority " + " and " − " operators are shown in Polish form.

Standard form	$3 + 4$
Polish form	$3\ 4\ +$
Standard form	$3 + 4 - 6$
Polish form	$3\ 4\ +\ 6\ -$
Standard form	$1 + 2 - 3 + 4 - 5 + 6 - 7 + 8 - 9$
Polish form	$1\ 2\ +\ 3\ -\ 4\ +\ 5\ -\ 6\ +\ 7\ -\ 8\ +\ 9\ -$

For these expressions the Polish form is quite similar to the standard form; the only difference is that operators appear after their two operands rather than between them. For these simple expressions there is no apparent advantage to Polish notation.

The real benefit of Polish strings is realized when parenthetical and priority structures are required for standard form presentation. Polish notation provides a convenient alternative to these structures. This is evident from the following examples.

Standard form	$3 * 2 + 4 = 10$
Polish form	$3\ 2\ *\ 4\ +$

$$\underbrace{3\ 2\ *}_{6}$$

$$\underbrace{\qquad\qquad}_{10}$$

Standard form $3 * (2 + 4) = 18$
Polish form $3 \underbrace{2\ 4\ +}\ *$

$$\underbrace{6}$$

$$18$$

Standard form $3 + 2 * 4 = 11$
Polish form $3 \underbrace{2\ 4\ *}\ +$

$$\underbrace{8}$$

$$11$$

Standard form $(3 + 2) * 4 = 20$
Polish form $\underbrace{3\ 2\ +}\ 4\ *$

$$\underbrace{5}$$

$$20$$

The order of operator evaluation and the operands to which each operator applies is determined simply by the position of operators in the Polish string.

Polish notation may be used for Boolean as well as arithmetic expressions. Examples of this application are

Standard form   NAME = JONES & AGE > 26
Polish form   NAME JONES = AGE 26 > &

Standard form   DEGREE = BA | DEGREE = BS & PROFESSION =
                  ENGINEER & (AGE > 35 | EXPERIENCE = SUPERVISOR)
Polish form   DEGREE BA = DEGREE BS = | PROFESSION
                  ENGINEER = & AGE 35 > EXPERIENCE SUPERVISOR
                  = | &

Even the most complicated expressions reduce to simple Polish forms. For example:

Standard form $[(3 + 2) * 5] - \{[(5 - 1)/(3 + 1)] * 3\}$
Polish form $3\ 2\ +\ 5\ *\ 5\ 1\ -\ 3\ 1\ +\ /\ 3\ *\ -$

The Polish form is still evaluated by application of the two simple rules: operators are applied in a left-to-right order, and operators are applied to the preceding two operands.

$$
\left.\begin{array}{l}
\left.\begin{array}{l}
\left.\begin{array}{l}
\left.\begin{array}{l}3 \\ 2 \\ +\end{array}\right\}5 \\ 5 \\ *\end{array}\right\}25 \\
\left.\begin{array}{l}
\left.\begin{array}{l}5 \\ \left.\begin{array}{l}1 \\ -\end{array}\right\} \\ \left.\begin{array}{l}3 \\ 1 \\ +\end{array}\right\}4 \\ /\end{array}\right\}4 \\ 3 \\ *\end{array}\right\}1 \\
-
\end{array}\right\}22
$$

3.3. Polish Evaluation Algorithm

It is not difficult to form a programing algorithm for evaluating Polish strings. To develop this algorithm let us look at the evaluation of our previous Polish string from a different standpoint. As each operation is performed the result will replace the operator and its two operands.

Operation 1	*Operation 2*	*Operation 3*	*Operation 4*
3 ⎫	5 ⎫	25	25
2 ⎬5	5 ⎬25	5 ⎫	4
+ ⎭	* ⎭	1 ⎬4	3 ⎫
5	5	− ⎭	1 ⎬4
*	1	3	+ ⎭
5	−	1	/
1	3	+	3
−	1	/	*
3	+	3	−
1	/	*	
+	3	−	
/	*		
3	−		
*			
−			

Operation 5	Operation 6	Operation 7	Value of string
25	25	25 ⎤	22
4 ⎤	1 ⎤	3 ⎬22	
4 ⎬1	3 ⎬3	− ⎦	
/ ⎦	* ⎦		
3	−		
*			
−			

Operators are evaluated in a left-to-right (in this case top-to-bottom) order. Each operator, when applied to the two preceding operands, produces a resultant operand. The resultant operand then replaces the operators and two operands used in the computation.

$$\left.\begin{array}{l} \text{operand} \\ \text{operand} \\ \text{operator} \end{array}\right\} \text{resultant operand}$$

This method of operation may be computationally effected by use of a stack table and by use of a cursor pointing to the current position in the Polish string. Operands are stripped from the string in a left-to-right order and placed in the stack table. When an operator is encountered in the string, it is applied to, and the result replaces, the last two operands in the stack. When the scan of the string is complete the stack table contains one entry: the value of the Polish string. This algorithm is flow charted as shown in Fig. 3.1.

Let us now formulate this algorithm in compiler-like language. In this formulation CURSOR will take on values like *1, 2, 3*, etc. STRING(I) will refer to the *i*th element of the Polish string. Therefore STRING(CURSOR) will refer to the Polish element indicated by the CURSOR. Our program will appear as follows.

(1)   CURSOR = 1
(2)   EMPTY(STACK)
(3)   IF STRING(CURSOR) = ENDSTRING THEN UNSTACK(VALUE),
      HALT
(4)   IF STRING(CURSOR) = OPERAND THEN STACK STRING(CURSOR),
      GO TO 12
(5)   UNSTACK(B)
(6)   UNSTACK(A)
(7)   IF STRING(CURSOR) = ' + ' THEN STACK(A + B), GO TO 12

(8) IF STRING(CURSOR) = ' − ' THEN STACK(A − B), GO TO 12
(9) IF STRING(CURSOR) = '*' THEN STACK(A * B), GO TO 12
(10) IF STRING(CURSOR) = '/' THEN STACK(A / B), GO TO 12
(11) IF STRING(CURSOR) = ' ↑ ' THEN STACK(A ↑ B)
(12) CURSOR = CURSOR + 1
(13) GO TO 3

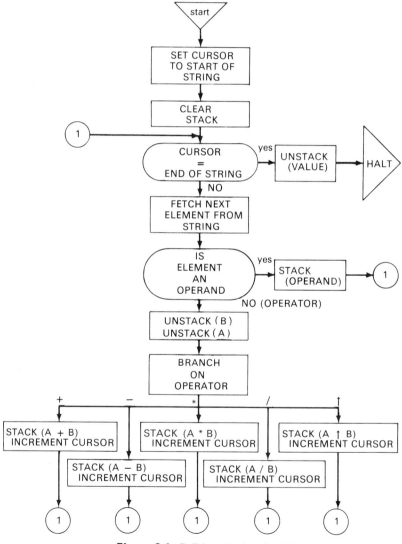

Figure 3.1. Polish evaluation algorithm.

Let us trace this program for the Polish string equivalent $6 * (5 - 2)$. The STRING would appear as

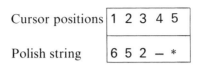

Cursor positions | 1 2 3 4 5

Polish string | 6 5 2 − *

(1)   CURSOR = 1
(2)   EMPTY(STACK)

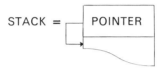

STACK = POINTER

(3)   IF STRING(1) = ENDSTRING ...
(4)   IF STRING(1) = OPERAND THEN STACK(6), GO TO 12

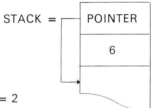

STACK = POINTER
6

(12) CURSOR = 2
(13) GO TO 3
(3)   IF STRING(2) = ENDSTRING ...
(4)   IF STRING(2) = OPERAND THEN STACK(5), GO TO 12

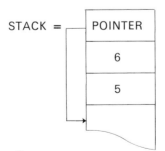

STACK = POINTER
6
5

(12) CURSOR = 3
(13) GO TO 3
(3)   IF STRING(3) = ENDSTRING ...
(4)   IF STRING(3) = OPERAND THEN STACK(2), GO TO 12

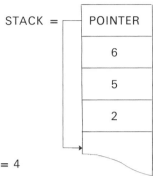

(12) CURSOR = 4
(13) GO TO 3
(3)   IF STRING(4) = ENDSTRING...
(4)   IF STRING(4) = OPERAND...
(5)   UNSTACK(B)
                B = 2

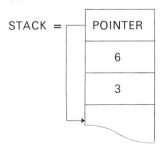

(6)   UNSTACK(A)
                A = 5

(7)   IF STRING(4) = ' + '...
(8)   IF STRING(4) = ' − ' THEN STACK(5 − 2), GO TO 12

(12) CURSOR = 5
(13) GO TO 3
(3)   IF STRING(5) = ENDSTRING...
(4)   IF STRING(5) = OPERAND...
(5)   UNSTACK(B)
              B = 3

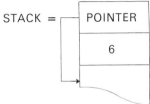

(6)   UNSTACK(A)
              A = 6

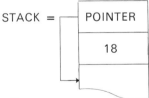

(7)   IF STRING(5) = ' + '...
(8)   IF STRING(5) = ' − '...
(9)   IF STRING(5) = '*' THEN STACK(6 * 3), GO TO 12

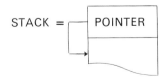

(12) CURSOR = 6
(13) GO TO 3
(3)   IF STRING(6) = ENDSTRING THEN UNSTACK(VALUE), HALT
              VALUE = 18

HALT

As can be seen the algorithm computed the proper VALUE.

3.4   Summary

Polish notation provides a convenient means for internal processing of Boolean and arithmetic expressions. We have seen what Polish strings look like and how they are evaluated. A later section of this book will present an algorithm for breaking a standard form expression into Polish form.

3.5
exercises

(1) What is the value of using Polish notation?

(2) What effect do operator priorities have in evaluating a standard form expression?

(3) What is the relation of the order of operands in a standard form expression to the order in a Polish form?

(4) Convert the following standard form expressions to Polish form.
 (a) $3 * 7 + 2$
 (b) $3 * (7 + 2)$
 (c) $3 + 2 * 7$
 (d) $A \& B | C$
 (e) $A \& (B | C)$
 (f) $3 + (7 * 4) \uparrow 2$
 In these conversions assume the following levels of operator priorities.

Priority	Operator
1	$\uparrow$
2	$*/$
3	$+-$
4	$\&|$

(5) Assuming the same priority structure as that of Question 4, show all possible Polish forms of the following expressions.
 (a) $3 + 7 - 6 * 4$
 (b) $3 + (7 - 6 * 4)$
 (c) $3 * 4 * 2 - 7$
 (d) $3 * 4 * (2 - 7)$

(6) In some languages a "¬" operator, standing for Boolean "not," is used. This operator applies to the single following operand. For example:

$$¬A$$
$$¬(A \mid B)$$

Assume the following priority structure.

Priority	Operator
1	¬
2	&|

Show the Polish forms of the following expressions.

(a) ¬A

(b) ¬A | B

(c) ¬(A | B)

(d) A & ¬(B | C)

(7) Flow chart an algorithm for evaluating Polish forms of Boolean expressions. Support &, |, and ¬ operators in this algorithm.

4

syntax directed methods

Syntax directed methods provide an analytical technique that is becoming more and more important in programming today, a technique with which all professional programmers should be familiar.

Programming sadly lacks the necessary production tools comparable to those employed in other professions. Pencil and paper, blackboard and chalk are still the basic means of program production. Once the original coding stage is reached, of course, the situation changes. Then assemblers, compilers, debugging aids, and other tools speed the completion of the work. But the essence of programming is in analysis and design, and here the programmer works basically with his unaided mind and hands against the problematic world.

Syntax directed methods provide a basic tool for formulating and structuring a system language. The notion of syntax is derived from the study of natural languages. Because of this, syntax is frequently associated with meaning or significance of words. This notion, however, is incorrect. Syntax is a study of language structure, not a study of the words themselves. A language syntax is a set of rules that dictates how the words, or basic elements, of the language are ordered to form meaningful phrases and statements.

The end product of the following sections is a technique for programming the syntax of an application language. As we will see, syntax directed programming not only simplifies the programming task itself, but also establishes a concrete framework for initial design and specification of the system: a standard and fixed reference for rigid clarification of the programming product.

4.1. Diagramming

As we learned in grammar school, an English sentence can be parsed by the technique of diagramming the sentence. For example, the sentence "THE CAT CLIMBS A TREE" may be diagrammed as shown in Fig. 4.1. Such a diagram displays the syntax (grammatical structure) of a sentence in a tree

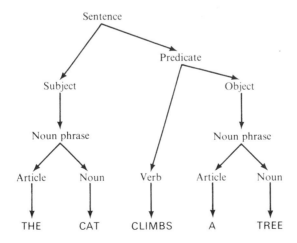

Figure 4.1. Sentence diagram.

fashion. Each node represents a component (or phrase) of the syntax. The uppercase words are the basic words (or primitives) of the language.

The general syntax of this type of sentence may be described in another way, as:

Sentence ← subject & predicate
Subject ← noun phrase
Noun phrase ← article & noun
Predicate ← verb & object
Object ← noun phrase
Verb ← CLIMBS
Article ← A | THE
Noun ← CAT | TREE

The arrow separates a syntactical component name from its definition. Definitions are made in terms of other components. The sign "&" concatenates components in a definition. For example a sentence is defined as a subject concatenated with a predicate. Both usually occur in an English sentence. The sign "|" separates alternative definitions of a component. For example, nouns are defined as either CAT *or* TREE. Of course there are other alternative nouns in the English language, but for this discussion we are only concerned with these two.

The rules we have set down describe a structure of an English sentence. Each rule is called a syntax equation; the set of all syntax rules is the syntax of the language. The important aspect of these syntax equations is they are not restricted to only one sentence. The rules dictate the structure for any sentence similar to the example given. Figure 4.2 shows such a sentence treated as in the previous example.

Let's try another example more closely related to syntax problems encountered in the computing world. An assembly language may be structured on three components: Label, Operation, and Operand. The statement START LOAD X1, LOC could then be diagrammed as in Fig. 4.3. The syntax equations for our assembler are then formulated.

Statement ← Label & Operation & Operand
Label ← Symbol
Operation ← LOAD | STORE | ADD etc.
Operand ← Register & Symbol
Register ← X1 | X2 | X3 | etc.
Symbol ← START | LOC | TAG   etc.

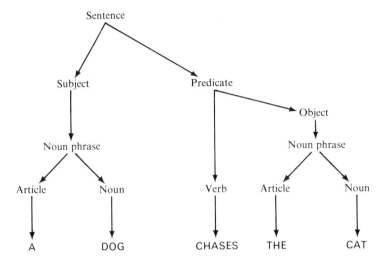

Figure 4.2. Sentence diagram.

4.2. Formal Syntax Definition

Syntax equations are used to specify an application language. When syntax equations are put to this use, a rigorous formal definition is required; we have to know exactly what rules the equations present. Not only must the syntax definition be precise, it must also be readily understandable. Therefore it is fitting we use a standard notation; namely, the Backus Naur form presentation.

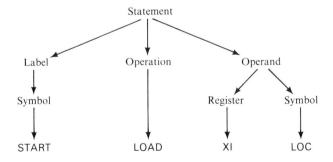

Figure 4.3. Statement diagram.

In Backus Naur form the symbol " :: = " is used to separate a syntactical component from its definition; this symbol replaces our arrow (←). Intermediate components are enclosed in brackets; for example, ⟨subject⟩, ⟨predicate⟩. The basic components are not enclosed in brackets; for example, THE, A, TREE, CAT. Alternate components in a definition are separated by the same vertical line "|." Our "&" sign, however, is not used; a space or a null is used to connect components in a definition.

Two of our previous equations are presented in Backus Naur form as

Predicate ← Verb & Object	(our form)
⟨predicate⟩ :: = ⟨verb⟩ ⟨object⟩	(Backus Naur)
Article ← THE | A	(our form)
⟨article⟩ :: = THE | A	(Backus Naur)

Our syntax for a simplified English grammar would then be expressed as

$$⟨sentence⟩ :: = ⟨subject⟩ ⟨predicate⟩$$
$$⟨subject⟩ :: = ⟨noun\ phrase⟩$$
$$⟨noun\ phrase⟩ :: = ⟨article⟩ ⟨noun⟩$$
$$⟨predicate⟩ :: = ⟨verb⟩ ⟨object⟩$$
$$⟨object⟩ :: = ⟨noun\ phrase⟩$$
$$⟨article⟩ :: = THE \mid A$$
$$⟨noun⟩ :: = CAT \mid TREE$$
$$⟨verb⟩ :: = CLIMBS$$

4.2.1. Order

When two components in a definition are concatenated they must appear in the order specified. Therefore, ⟨sentence⟩ :: = ⟨subject⟩ ⟨predicate⟩ dictates that the subject must always precede the predicate.

4.2.2. Combination

Alternative concatenations may be used in a component definition. For example:

$$⟨sentence⟩ :: = ⟨subject⟩ ⟨predicate⟩ \mid ⟨predicate⟩ ⟨subject⟩$$

would dictate that a sentence is either formed from a subject followed by a predicate or from a predicate followed by a subject. This presents a more viable sentence structure in English grammar.

4.2.3. Recursion

Backus Naur permits a component to be defined partially in terms of itself. For example:

⟨noun phrase⟩ ::= ⟨adjective⟩ ⟨noun phrase⟩|⟨noun⟩
⟨adjective⟩ ::= BIG | BAD
⟨noun⟩ :: = BEAR

These equations define a ⟨noun phrase⟩ as a ⟨noun⟩ preceded by zero or more ⟨adjectives⟩. Examples of legal noun phrases are

BEAR
BIG BEAR
BAD BEAR
BIG BAD BEAR
BAD BIG BEAR
BIG BIG BEAR
BAD BAD BEAR

4.2.4. Common Phrases

The value and purpose of syntax equations is to build an overall syntax on common phrases and components, actively seeking and maintaining a consistency throughout the application language. For example, in a FORTRAN compiler the syntax equations for each FORTRAN statement would reference a common component for arithmetic expressions. Two such statements would be the DO statement and the ASSIGNMENT statement. Examples of these statements are

DO 10 I = 1, 10
DO 10 I = 2, 10, 2
X = 2 * (6 + K)
Y = 7 * L + 4 * X

Syntax equations for these statements might be written as

$\langle$statement$\rangle$ :: = $\langle$do$\rangle$ | $\langle$assign$\rangle$
$\langle$do$\rangle$ :: = DO $\langle$integer$\rangle$ $\langle$variable$\rangle$ = $\langle$exp$\rangle$, $\langle$exp$\rangle$, $\langle$exp$\rangle$
$\langle$assign$\rangle$ :: = $\langle$variable$\rangle$ = $\langle$exp$\rangle$
$\langle$variable$\rangle$ :: = I | J | K | L | . . .
$\langle$exp$\rangle$ :: = . . .

This use of common phrases first introduces a consistency in the application language, secondly insures this consistency is maintained in implementation, and thirdly simplifies the task of implementation.

4.3. Automatic Parsing

As was shown in previous sections, syntax equations may be used to diagram
and formally specify an application language. A second use of syntax equations is in programming the application. A program can be written to break
down, or parse, the application language by stepping through, or interpreting, the syntax equations. This parsing program analyzes a statement in the
application language by tracing through the diagrammed structure of the
syntax equations. Let us, at this time, take a look at how such a program
might be formulated.

Consider the tree structure represented by our syntax equations. To
parse a statement we have to associate that statement with the syntax tree.
There are two basic methods for effecting this association.

(1) Bottom to top : Start with the basic components of a statement and
    work up the syntax tree.
(2) Top to bottom : Start with the entire sentence at the top of the tree
    and work down to basic components.

4.3.1. Bottom to Top Parsing

Bottom to top parsing is conceptually easier to grasp. Individual words
in the sentence are matched against basic definitions in a syntax tree. As
these basic entities are recognized they are collected and transformed into

higher order components. For example, recall the equations for our subset of the English grammar.

$$\langle\text{sentence}\rangle :: = \langle\text{subject}\rangle \langle\text{predicate}\rangle$$
$$\langle\text{subject}\rangle :: = \langle\text{noun phrase}\rangle$$
$$\langle\text{noun phrase}\rangle :: = \langle\text{article}\rangle \langle\text{noun}\rangle$$
$$\langle\text{predicate}\rangle :: = \langle\text{verb}\rangle \langle\text{object}\rangle$$
$$\langle\text{object}\rangle :: = \langle\text{noun phrase}\rangle$$
$$\langle\text{article}\rangle :: = \text{THE} \mid \text{A}$$
$$\langle\text{noun}\rangle :: = \text{CAT} \mid \text{TREE}$$
$$\langle\text{verb}\rangle :: = \text{CLIMBS}$$

In bottom to top parsing of "THE CAT CLIMBS A TREE" the first associations discovered would be

$$\text{THE} \rightarrow \text{article } \#1$$
$$\text{CAT} \rightarrow \text{noun } \#1$$
$$\text{CLIMBS} \rightarrow \text{verb}$$
$$\text{A} \rightarrow \text{article } \#2$$
$$\text{TREE} \rightarrow \text{noun } \#2$$

Having matched all first order components of the sentence, these components would then be collected to form second order components.

$$\text{article } \#1 \text{ \& noun } \#1 \rightarrow \text{noun phrase } \#1$$
$$\text{article } \#2 \text{ \& noun } \#2 \rightarrow \text{noun phrase } \#2$$

In the next stage

$$\text{noun phrase } \#1 \rightarrow \text{subject}$$
$$\text{noun phrase } \#2 \rightarrow \text{object}$$

Then

$$\text{verb \& object} \rightarrow \text{predicate}$$

Finally

$$\text{subject \& predicate} \rightarrow \text{sentence}$$

4.3.2. Top to Bottom Parsing

Top to bottom parsing is a procedure that creates goals and subgoals in attempting to relate a statement to its syntax environment. When checking out subgoals, false starts and improper branches are tested and discarded until the proper subgoal is achieved. As in our grammar example

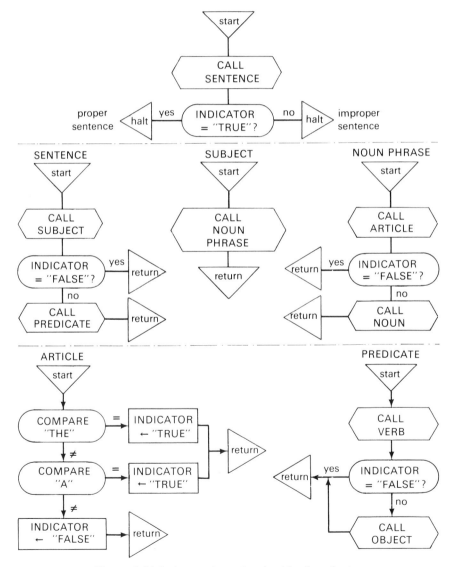

Figure 4.4 (a). Automatic parsing algorithm flow chart.

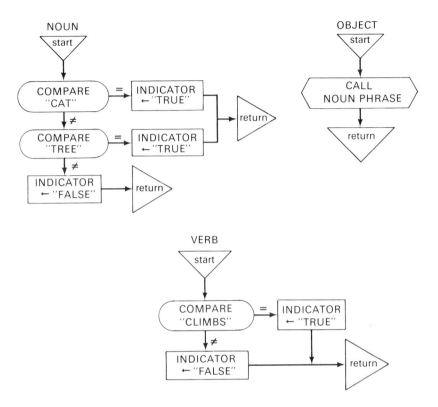

Figure 4.4(b). Automatic parsing algorithm flow chart.

the major goal is ⟨sentence⟩. To effect this goal subgoals of ⟨subject⟩ and ⟨predicate⟩ must be realized; these, in turn, have their own subgoals. The parsing procedure must, at each juncture in the syntax structure, examine subgoals. If the required subgoals are realized, then the encompassing higher goal is, by definition, realized. If the subgoals are not realized the higher goal is discarded. This sequence of testing, discarding, and finally realizing goals is propagated down through the syntax tree until either all basic components have been gathered into higher level components or until the sentence is proven in error.

4.3.3. Computer Based Parsing

We will now formulate a top to bottom parsing algorithm. The only requirements are that the algorithm first keep track of where it is in the syntax tree and secondly categorize the subgoals on a "true/false" basis. To illustrate how this can be done consider a small program to parse our "cat climbs tree" sentence.

Remember the two requirements of a top to bottom parsing algorithm: the program must keep track of where it is in the syntax tree, and subgoals must be categorized on a "true/false" basis. For this example we will incorporate the syntax tree right into the program; this satisfies the tracking requirements. The second requirement will be satisfied by maintaining a "true/false" program flag. To present the algorithm (Fig. 4.4) consider the following computer-like operations.

CALL Subroutine: transfers control to the specified subroutine.

RETURN: returns control from whence the subroutine was called.

COMPARE Word: looks at the next item in the sentence. If it is the same as "Word", then advance the scan so that any subsequent COMPARE will reference the next sentence item.

In compiler-like coding this algorithm appears as

Statement
number   *Operation*

(1)		CALL SENTENCE
(2)		IF INDICATOR = 'FALSE', HALT (IMPROPER SENTENCE)
(3)		HALT (PROPER SENTENCE)
(4)	SENTENCE:	CALL SUBJECT
(5)		IF INDICATOR = 'FALSE', RETURN
(6)		CALL PREDICATE
(7)		RETURN
(8)	SUBJECT:	CALL NOUNPHRASE
(9)		RETURN
(10)	NOUNPHRASE:	CALL ARTICLE
(11)		IF INDICATOR = 'FALSE', RETURN
(12)		CALL NOUN
(13)		RETURN
(14)	PREDICATE:	CALL VERB
(15)		IF INDICATOR = 'FALSE', RETURN
(16)		CALL OBJECT
(17)		RETURN
(18)	OBJECT:	CALL NOUNPHRASE
(19)		RETURN
(20)	ARTICLE:	IF COMPARE 'THE', INDICATOR = 'TRUE', RETURN

Statement
number   *Operation*

(21)   IF COMPARE 'A', INDICATOR = 'TRUE', RETURN
(22)   INDICATOR = 'FALSE'
(23)   RETURN
(24) NOUN: IF COMPARE 'CAT', INDICATOR = 'TRUE', RETURN
(25)   IF COMPARE 'TREE', INDICATOR = 'TRUE', RETURN
(26)   INDICATOR = 'FALSE'
(27)   RETURN
(28) VERB: IF COMPARE 'CLIMBS', INDICATOR = 'TRUE', RETURN
(29)   INDICATOR = 'FALSE'
(30)   RETURN

Let us put this program to work parsing THE CAT CLIMBS A TREE. If we designate WORD(I) as the *i*th word in the sentence we can trace the operations of the program.

Statement
number   *Operation*

(1)   CALL SENTENCE
(4)   CALL SUBJECT
(8)   CALL NOUN PHRASE
(10)   CALL ARTICLE
(20)   COMPARE WORD(1) = 'THE'
               INDICATOR = 'TRUE'
               RETURN
(11)   IF INDICATOR = 'FALSE'...
(12)   CALL NOUN
(24)   COMPARE WORD(2) = 'CAT'
               INDICATOR = 'TRUE'
               RETURN
(13)   RETURN
(9)   RETURN
(5)   IF INDICATOR = 'FALSE'...
(6)   CALL PREDICATE
(14)   CALL VERB
(28)   COMPARE WORD(3) = 'CLIMBS'
               INDICATOR = 'TRUE'
               RETURN
(15)   IF INDICATOR = 'FALSE'...
(16)   CALL OBJECT
(18)   CALL NOUN PHRASE

Statement
number   *Operation*

```
(10)    CALL ARTICLE
(20)    IF COMPARE WORD(4) = 'THE'...
(21)    COMPARE WORD(4) = 'A'
            INDICATOR = 'TRUE'
            RETURN
(11)    IF INDICATOR = 'FALSE'...
(12)    CALL NOUN
(24)    IF COMPARE WORD(5) = 'CAT'...
(25)    COMPARE WORD(5) = 'TREE'
            INDICATOR = 'TRUE'
            RETURN
(13)    RETURN
(19)    RETURN
(17)    RETURN
(7)     RETURN
(2)     IF INDICATOR = 'FALSE'...
(3)     HALT (PROPER SENTENCE)
```

We have now parsed the sentence (in this case checked for grammatical errors). Because the syntax was embedded in the program, the subroutine calls kept track of current positions in the syntax tree; they acted as a memory of which goals and which subgoals were being examined. The true/false indicator then specified whether or not these goals were realized. This technique parses the sentence in a single left-to-right scan of the text. Although there were some false starts, the overall parsing flow was fairly good. But more important, the program permitted a consistent breakdown of the sentence into common phrases and subphrases.

4.4. Syntax Problems in Automatic Parsing

As we have seen, an automatic parsing algorithm can be based on a set of syntax equations. When drawing up such an algorithm the writer must be aware of certain restrictions. Two such restrictions are "ordering of alternatives" and "circular definitions."

4.4.1. Ordering of Alternatives

The ordering of alternatives in the syntax equations of an automatic parsing algorithm may be of significance. For example, consider the following syntax for noun phrase.

⟨noun phrase⟩ :: = ⟨adjective list⟩ ⟨noun⟩ | ⟨noun⟩
⟨adjective list⟩ :: = ⟨adjective⟩ ⟨adjective list⟩ | ⟨adjective⟩
⟨adjective⟩ :: = BIG | BAD
⟨noun⟩ :: = BEAR

An algorithm based on this syntax will properly parse any of the "big bad bear" class of noun phrases. However, consider the effect of reordering the adjective list syntax equation.

⟨noun phrase⟩ :: = ⟨adjective list⟩ ⟨noun⟩ | ⟨noun⟩
⟨adjective list⟩ :: = ⟨adjective⟩ | ⟨adjective⟩ ⟨adjective list⟩
⟨adjective⟩ :: = BIG | BAD
⟨noun⟩ :: = BEAR

An algorithm based on this syntax may not recognize BIG BAD BEAR as a valid noun phrase. Let us assume the algorithm processes syntactical alternatives in a left-to-right order. The first alternative of ⟨adjective list⟩ would be ⟨adjective⟩. The second alternative would be ⟨adjective⟩ ⟨adjective list⟩. Now in processing BIG BAD BEAR, the algorithm would categorize BIG, itself, as an ⟨adjective list⟩. The second adjective, BAD, would never be recognized.

4.4.2. Circular Definitions

When we talked of recursive definitions we said a component may be defined partially in terms of itself. Here, partial is the critical qualification, for a component cannot be defined entirely in terms of itself. For example ⟨adjective list⟩ :: = ⟨adjective list⟩ is obviously a meaningless circular definition. However there are indirect circular definitions that are not so obvious.

⟨adjective list⟩ :: = ⟨multiple⟩ | ⟨single⟩
⟨single⟩ :: = ⟨adjective⟩
⟨multiple⟩ :: = ⟨adjective⟩ ⟨adjective list⟩ | ⟨adjective list⟩

Consider a parsing algorithm based on this syntax. It will process the adjective list properly. However, when the list is exhausted the equations become circular. For example, BIG BAD BEAR is processed through the ⟨multiple⟩ equation. After BAD is recognized the multiple equation uses its second alternative of adjective list, which returns to where the equation was called only to be called again and again.

4.5. Summary

Syntax directed methods provide a tool for the structure and processing of a programming language. With these methods the language structure is defined by a set of syntax equations. Each equation declares the proper forms for one segment or subset of the language. From the equations it is possible to create a programming algorithm to check a sentence for valid syntax. As the algorithm is executed it matches segments and subsets of the sentence to syntax structures imbedded in algorithm statements. The algorithm fits a sentence to its syntactical definition.

4.6
exercises

(1) What are the advantages of a formal syntax definition?

(2) Consider the following syntax equations.

⟨COLOR⟩ :: = ⟨LIST1⟩ ⟨HUE⟩ | ⟨HUE⟩
⟨LIST1⟩ :: = ⟨QUALIFIER1⟩ ⟨LIST1⟩ | ⟨QUALIFIER1⟩
⟨HUE⟩ :: = ⟨GREEN⟩ | ⟨BLUE⟩
⟨GREEN⟩ :: = ⟨LIST2⟩ GREEN | GREEN
⟨LIST2⟩ :: = ⟨QUALIFIER2⟩ ⟨LIST2⟩ | ⟨QUALIFIER2⟩
⟨BLUE⟩ :: = ⟨LIST3⟩ BLUE | BLUE
⟨LIST3⟩ :: = ⟨QUALIFIER3⟩ ⟨LIST3⟩ | ⟨QUALIFIER3⟩
⟨QUALIFIER1⟩ :: = LIGHT | DARK | DEEP | PALE
⟨QUALIFIER2⟩ :: = SEA | EMERALD
⟨QUALIFIER3⟩ :: = MIDNIGHT | SKY | ROBIN'S EGG

Which of the following are legal?
(a) BLUE
(b) DARK BLUE
(c) DARK DARK PALE BLUE
(d) DARK MIDNIGHT SKY BLUE
(e) MIDNIGHT DARK BLUE
(f) ROBIN'S EGG BLUE
(g) EMERALD SEA GREEN
(h) EMERALD DARK GREEN
(i) DARK LIGHT GREEN

(3) Write syntax equations for the assembly or compiler language you are most familiar with. In this syntax do not break down the forms of arithmetic and Boolean expressions.

(4) Describe, in your own words, a process for automatic parsing based on syntax equations.

(5) What are two problems that may arise when basing a parsing algorithm on syntax equations?

5
programming
languages

In previous sections examples for our development of syntax analysis were drawn from natural languages. In this section syntax analysis will be applied to programming languages. We will first construct syntax equations for describing a simple programming language; then the equations will be translated to computer algorithms to show how processing of the language is automated. Many of the techniques required for this discussion have been covered in previous sections; however, these will be supplemented by new methods and techniques as the need arises.

5.1. Symbol Declaration

Our discussion will begin with the basic elements of a programming language. These include identifiers (labels and variables), which will be grouped in the general category called "symbols." In our programming language a symbol is a string of alphanumeric characters. The first character of the string must be alphabetic. Examples of legal symbols are

TAG
L2
T

Examples of illegal symbols are

TA%G   (nonalphanumeric character)
2L   (leading character nonalphabetic)

Syntax equations for a symbol are constructed as follows.

$$\langle symbol \rangle :: = \langle alpha \rangle \langle string \rangle \mid \langle alpha \rangle$$
$$\langle string \rangle :: = \langle alphanumeric \rangle \langle string \rangle \mid \langle alphanumeric \rangle$$
$$\langle alphanumeric \rangle :: = \langle alpha \rangle \mid \langle numeric \rangle$$
$$\langle alpha \rangle :: = A \mid B \mid C \ldots \mid X \mid Y \mid Z$$
$$\langle numeric \rangle :: = 1 \mid 2 \mid 3 \mid \ldots \mid 8 \mid 9 \mid 0$$

A SYMBOL is defined as an alpha character followed by an optional STRING of alphanumeric characters. The STRING equation specifies repeated occurrence of alphanumeric characters by recursion. The final character of STRING terminates the recursion.

To automate the detection of a symbol this syntax structure could be imbedded in a computer algorithm. The algorithm would scan a character stream input to the computer through the following basic operations.

CALL subroutine: Transfer control to a subroutine of the algorithm.
RETURN: Return control from a subroutine.
COMPARE "character": Compare the next character of the input stream to the specified digit. If a match is made advance the scan so that a subsequent COMPARE will examine the next character of the stream.

As in previous algorithms a true/false INDICATOR will be kept to direct the flow of control through the algorithm structure. Our SYMBOL algorithm appears as follows.

```
SYMBOL:          CALL ALPHA
                 IF INDICATOR = 'FALSE' THEN RETURN
                   (IMPROPER SYMBOL)
                 CALL STRING
                 IF INDICATOR = 'FALSE' THEN RETURN
                   (PROPER  −1 CHARACTER SYMBOL)
                 RETURN (PROPER MULTIPLE CHARACTER
                   SYMBOL)
STRING:          CALL ALPHANUMERIC
                 IF INDICATOR = 'FALSE' THEN RETURN
STRING1:         CALL ALPHANUMERIC
                 IF INDICATOR = 'TRUE' THEN CALL STRING1
                 INDICATOR = 'TRUE'
                 RETURN
ALPHANUMERIC:    CALL ALPHA
                 IF INDICATOR = 'TRUE' THEN RETURN
                 CALL NUMERIC
                 RETURN
ALPHA:           IF COMPARE 'A' THEN INDICATOR = 'TRUE',
                   RETURN
                 IF COMPARE 'B' THEN INDICATOR = 'TRUE',
                   RETURN
                       .
                       .
                       .
                 IF COMPARE 'Z' THEN INDICATOR = 'TRUE',
                   RETURN
                 INDICATOR = 'FALSE', RETURN
NUMERIC:         IF COMPARE '1' THEN INDICATOR = 'TRUE',
                   RETURN
                 IF COMPARE '2' THEN INDICATOR = 'TRUE',
                   RETURN
                       .
                       .
                       .
                 IF COMPARE '0' THEN INDICATOR = 'TRUE'
                   RETURN
                 INDICATOR = 'FALSE', RETURN
```

Unfortunately, several syntax structures are required for the definition of an entity as simple and basic as a symbol. This is because of the recursion required to define a repeating set of alphanumeric characters. To simplify

the description of repeating syntactical entities we will introduce a new
operator into our formal syntax. The operator "∫[...]" will specify that
all syntax items enclosed by brackets are to be repeated zero or more times.
Incorporation of this operator into our SYMBOL syntax produces the
following set of equations.

$$\langle\text{symbol}\rangle ::= \langle\text{alpha}\rangle \int [\, \langle\text{alpha}\rangle \,|\, \langle\text{numeric}\rangle\,]$$
$$\langle\text{alpha}\rangle ::= A \,|\, B \,|\, C \,|\, ... \,|\, X \,|\, Y \,|\, Z$$
$$\langle\text{numeric}\rangle ::= 1 \,|\, 2 \,|\, 3 \,|\, ... \,|\, 8 \,|\, 9 \,|\, 0$$

This syntax, equivalent to the previous, declares a symbol as an alpha
character followed by zero or more alphanumeric characters.

This syntax simplifies our automated algorithm for detecting a symbol.
We have eliminated the STRING and ALPHANUMERIC subroutines.

```
SYMBOL:     CALL ALPHA
            IF INDICATOR = 'FALSE' THEN RETURN (IMPROPER
            SYMBOL)
SYMBOL1:    CALL ALPHA
            IF INDICATOR = 'TRUE' THEN CALL SYMBOL1
            CALL NUMERIC
            IF INDICATOR = 'TRUE' THEN CALL SYMBOL1
            RETURN (PROPER SYMBOL)
ALPHA:      IF COMPARE 'A' THEN INDICATOR = 'TRUE', RETURN
            IF COMPARE 'B' THEN INDICATOR = 'TRUE', RETURN
                        .
                        .
                        .
            IF COMPARE 'Z' THEN INDICATOR = 'TRUE', RETURN
            INDICATOR = 'FALSE', RETURN
NUMERIC:    IF COMPARE '1' THEN INDICATOR = 'TRUE', RETURN
            IF COMPARE '2' THEN INDICATOR = 'TRUE', RETURN
                        .
                        .
                        .
            IF COMPARE '0' THEN INDICATOR = 'TRUE', RETURN
            INDICATOR = 'FALSE', RETURN
```

In many programming languages the length of a symbol is fixed. For
example, in FORTRAN a label or variable may be at most six characters
long; in COBOL thirty-two. Such limits should be expressed by the syntax
of the programming language. To allow limit declaration we will add
optional upper and lower limit repetition counts to the repetition operator.
As an example, $\int_0^5 [\, ... \,]$ declares zero to five occurrences of those items

enclosed by brackets; the syntax equations for a FORTRAN symbol would then appear as follows.

$$\langle\text{symbol}\rangle ::= \langle\text{alpha}\rangle \int_0^5 [\,\langle\text{alpha}\rangle \mid \langle\text{numeric}\rangle\,]$$
$$\langle\text{alpha}\rangle ::= A \mid B \mid C \mid \ldots \mid X \mid Y \mid Z$$
$$\langle\text{numeric}\rangle ::= 1 \mid 2 \mid 3 \mid \ldots \mid 8 \mid 9 \mid 0$$

5.2. Constant Declaration

In most programming languages arithmetic constants are used. For our present discussion we will consider integer and decimal constants. Examples of each are.

Integer	Decimal
7	2.7
26412	.6143
0	14.0

The rules for forming integer and decimal constants are

Integer :   A string of numeric characters
Decimal :
   (1) A string of numeric characters followed by a decimal point and a numeric string
   (2) A decimal point followed by a numeric string

These rules may be summarized by syntax equations.

$$\langle\text{constant}\rangle ::= \langle\text{decimal}\rangle \mid \langle\text{integer}\rangle$$
$$\langle\text{decimal}\rangle ::= \langle\text{integer}\rangle \langle\text{fraction}\rangle \mid \langle\text{fraction}\rangle$$
$$\langle\text{fraction}\rangle ::= .\,\langle\text{integer}\rangle$$
$$\langle\text{integer}\rangle ::= \langle\text{numeric}\rangle \int [\,\langle\text{numeric}\rangle\,]$$
$$\langle\text{numeric}\rangle ::= 0 \mid 1 \mid 2 \mid 3 \mid \ldots \mid 8 \mid 9$$

Using our basic computational operations a computer algorithm could also be formed to detect an arithmetic constant.

```
CONSTANT:  CALL DECIMAL
           IF INDICATOR = 'FALSE' THEN CALL INTEGER
           IF INDICATOR = 'FALSE' THEN RETURN (IMPROPER
           CONSTANT)
```

```
                RETURN (PROPER CONSTANT)
DECIMAL:        CALL INTEGER
                CALL FRACTION
                RETURN
FRACTION:       IF COMPARE '.' THEN CALL INTEGER, RETURN
                INDICATOR = 'FALSE'
                RETURN
INTEGER:        CALL NUMERIC
                IF INDICATOR = 'FALSE' THEN RETURN
INTEGER1:       CALL NUMERIC
                IF INDICATOR = 'TRUE' THEN CALL INTEGER1
                INDICATOR = 'TRUE'
                RETURN
```

5.3. Expression Declaration

Now that we have the definition for SYMBOL and CONSTANT, we will examine the manner in which these items are combined to form expressions. First to be considered will be simple expressions using only the addition " $+$ " and subtraction " $-$ " operators. Examples of such expressions are

```
X − 4
RATE + TIME − 6
LENGTH + WIDTH +HEIGHT
X + 1 − Y
```

Symbols and constants become the *operands* to which these operators are applied. The syntax prescribing legal forms for combining operators and operands appears as follows.

$\langle$expression$\rangle$ :: = $\langle$operand$\rangle$ $\int$ [$\langle$operator$\rangle$ $\langle$operand$\rangle$]
$\langle$operator$\rangle$ :: = '+'|'−'
$\langle$operand$\rangle$ :: = $\langle$symbol$\rangle$ | $\langle$constant$\rangle$

This syntax structure may be imbedded in a computer algorithm as follows.

```
(1)  EXPRESSION:    CALL OPERAND
(2)                 IF INDICATOR = 'FALSE' THEN RETURN
                    (IMPROPER EXPRESSION)
```

```
(3)  EXPRESSION1:   CALL OPERATOR
(4)                 IF INDICATOR = 'FALSE' THEN RETURN
                    (PROPER EXPRESSION)
(5)                 CALL OPERAND
(6)                 IF INDICATOR = 'FALSE' THEN RETURN
                    (IMPROPER EXPRESSION)
(7)                 CALL EXPRESSION1
(8)  OPERATOR:      IF COMPARE ' +' THEN INDICATOR =
                    'TRUE', RETURN
(9)                 IF COMPARE ' −' THEN INDICATOR =
                    'TRUE', RETURN
(10)                INDICATOR = 'FALSE'
(11)                RETURN
(12) OPERAND:       CALL SYMBOL
(13)                IF INDICATOR = 'TRUE', THEN RETURN
(14)                CALL CONSTANT
(15)                RETURN
```

The algorithm accepts a character stream input to the computer. The stream is scanned for proper expression syntax, and the result (legal or illegal) is indicated by the indicator setting. At all times the scan position is maintained by the COMPARE cursor. When a COMPARE results in a match, the cursor is advanced; no match, and the cursor remains as positioned. To trace the flow of this algorithm the scan position must be kept in mind. Consider an expression example previously given.

$$X + 1 - Y$$

Position	Expression
1	X
2	+
3	1
4	−
5	Y

The initial setting for the COMPARE cursor is at scan position 1. A trace of the algorithm shows the advancement of this cursor as related to the number of the statement currently in execution. Execution begins at statement 1.

Statement
executed *Operation*
(1)   Control is transferred to OPERAND.
(12)   The symbol subroutine is called.
           Here X is detected, INDICATOR is set to TRUE, and CURSOR is advanced to
           position 2.
(13)   Return to statement 2.
(2)   No action taken.
(3)   Control is transferred to OPERATOR.
(8)   In position 2 the " + " is detected,
           CURSOR ← 3, INDICATOR ← TRUE,
           and control is returned to statement 4.
(4)   No action.
(5)   Control is transferred to OPERAND.
(12)   The symbol subroutine finds no symbol in position 3. It sets INDICATOR to
           FALSE and returns.
(13)   No action.
(14)   The constant routine is called. Here the constant (1) is detected in position 3.
           INDICATOR is set to TRUE, and CURSOR is advanced to position 4 before
           returning.
(15)   Return to statement 6.
(6)   No action.
(7)   Control is transferred to EXPRESSION1.
(3)   Control is transferred to OPERATOR.
(8)   Since there is no " + " in position 4, no action is taken.
(9)   The " − " is recognized in position 4, CURSOR ← 5, INDICATOR ← TRUE,
           and control is returned to statement 4.
(4)   No action.
(5)   Control is transferred to OPERAND.
(12)   The symbol subroutine is called. Here Y is detected at position 5, CURSOR ←
           6, and INDICATOR ← TRUE.
(13)   Control is returned to statement 6.
(6)   No action.
(7)   Control is transferred to EXPRESSION1.
(3)   Control is transferred to OPERATOR.
(8)   A " + " is not found at position 6.
(9)   A " − " is not found at position 6.
(10)   INDICATOR FALSE
(11)   Return to statement 4.
(4)   HALT (PROPER EXPRESSION)

This basic algorithm and its related syntax provide a starting point for
discussion of expressions. They will be expanded and modified as new
formats are added to the expression syntax. The first such format will be
parenthetical expressions; we will permit the use of parentheses in forming

an expression. For example,

$$4 - (7 + 2)$$
$$3 + (2 - (4 + 6))$$

In looking at these expressions we see that the parentheses enclose a sub-expression; the subexpression is used as a single operand. For example, 4 − (7 + 2) breaks down to the form 4 − OPERAND, where OPERAND = SUBEXPRESSION (7 + 2). In other words a sub-expression may be thought of as a special type of operand. This concept is evident in the following syntax.

$\langle$expression$\rangle$ :: = $\langle$operand$\rangle$ $\int$ [$\langle$operator$\rangle$ $\langle$operand$\rangle$]
$\langle$operator$\rangle$ :: = $'+'|'−'$
$\langle$operand$\rangle$ :: = $\langle$symbol$\rangle$ | $\langle$constant$\rangle$ | $\langle$subexpression$\rangle$
$\langle$subexpression$\rangle$ :: = ($\langle$expression$\rangle$)

Note that the syntax for parenthetical expressions is recursive. As our expression syntax is expanded we will see more and more recursion. As the syntax equations become recursive so must the corresponding computing algorithms. In preparation for this we will formulate a recursive algorithm for the above syntax.

To support recursive subroutines our algorithm must stack all calling addresses. The stack then forms a trace of where subsequent returns are to be made. The stacking procedure will be incorporated into CALL and RETURN operations of the computer algorithm.

CALL subroutine: Stack current statement number, then pass control to the designated subroutine.

RETURN: Unstack statement number, then return control to invoking call.

In addition to CALL and RETURN, a GO TO operation will be used to transfer control without stacking.

Now the algorithm for our parenthetical expression syntax will not explicitly show return stacking. The stacking will be implicitly imbedded in the CALL and RETURN operations. The algorithm will be initially called by a CALL EXPRESSION operation; the statements of this initial operation will be numbered i1 through i3.

(i1)		CALL EXPRESSION
(i2)		IF INDICATOR = 'FALSE' THEN HALT
		(IMPROPER EXPRESSION)
(i3)		HALT (PROPER EXPRESSION)
(1)	EXPRESSION:	CALL OPERAND
(2)		IF INDICATOR = 'FALSE' THEN RETURN
(3)	EXPRESSION1:	CALL OPERATOR
(4)		IF INDICATOR = 'FALSE' THEN
		INDICATOR = 'TRUE', RETURN
(5)		CALL OPERAND
(6)		IF INDICATOR = 'FALSE', THEN RETURN
(7)		GO TO EXPRESSION1
(8)	OPERATOR:	IF COMPARE ' + ' THEN INDICATOR =
		'TRUE', RETURN
(9)		IF COMPARE ' − ' THEN INDICATOR =
		'TRUE', RETURN
(10)		INDICATOR = 'FALSE' THEN RETURN
(11)	OPERAND:	CALL SYMBOL
(12)		IF INDICATOR = 'TRUE' THEN RETURN
(13)		CALL CONSTANT
(14)		IF INDICATOR = 'TRUE' THEN RETURN
(15)		CALL SUBEXPRESSION
(16)		RETURN
(17)	SUBEXPRESSION:	IF NO COMPARE '(' THEN INDICATOR =
		'FALSE', RETURN
(18)		CALL EXPRESSION
(19)		IF INDICATOR = 'FALSE' THEN RETURN
(20)		IF COMPARE ')' THEN INDICATOR =
		'TRUE', RETURN
(21)		INDICATOR = 'FALSE', RETURN

Let us trace the parsing of $4 - (7 + 2)$ through this algorithm.

Position	Expression
1	4
2	−
3	(
4	7
5	+
6	2
7	)

In the trace attention will be focused on three things: the recursion stack, CURSOR position, and INDICATOR. The trace will begin at statement i1.

Result

Statement executed	Action	INDICATOR	CURSOR position	Statement numbers in return stack
(i1)	Call expression	not applicable	1	i1
(1)	Call operand			i1, 1
(11)	No symbol found at position 1	FALSE		
(12)	No action			
(13)	Constant(4) detected at position 1	TRUE	2	
(14)	Return to statement 1			i1
(2)	No action			
(3)	Call operator			i1, 3
(8)	No action			
(9)	Operator (−) detected at position 2	TRUE	3	
	Return to statement 3			i1
(4)	No action			
(5)	Call operand			i1, 5
(11)	No symbol found at position 3	FALSE		
(12)	No action			
(13)	No constant found at position 3	FALSE		
(14)	No action			
(15)	Call subexpression			i1, 5, 15
(17)	"(" found at position 3		4	
(18)	Call expression			i1, 5, 15, 18
(1)	Call operand			i1, 5, 15, 18, 1
(11)	No symbol found at position 4	FALSE		
(12)	No action			
(13)	Constant(7) found at position 5	TRUE	5	
(14)	Return to statement 1			i1, 5, 15, 18
(2)	No action			
(3)	Call operator			i1, 5, 15, 18, 3
(8)	Operator (+) found at position 5	TRUE	6	
	Return to statement 3			i1, 5, 15, 18
(4)	No action			
(5)	Call operand			i1, 5, 15, 18, 5
(11)	No symbol found at position 6	FALSE		
(12)	No action			
(13)	Constant(2) found at position 6	TRUE	7	

Result

Statement executed	Action	INDICATOR	CURSOR position	Statement numbers in return stack
(14)	Return to statement 5			i1, 5, 15, 18
(6)	No action			
(7)	GO TO 3			
(3)	Call operator			i1, 5, 15, 18, 3
(8)	No action			
(9)	No action			
(10)	Return to statement 3	FALSE		i1, 5, 15, 18
(4)	Return to statement 18	TRUE		i1, 5, 15
(19)	No action			
(20)	")" found at position 7	TRUE	8	
	Return to statement 15			i1, 5
(16)	Return to statement 5			i1
(6)	No action			
(7)	GO TO 3			
(3)	Call operator			i1, 3
(8)	No action			
(9)	No action			
(10)	Return to statement 3	FALSE		i1
(4)	Return to statement i1	TRUE		empty
(i2)	No action			
(i3)	Halt (proper expression)			

This completes the trace of the parsing algorithm.

A further expansion of expression syntax is required to support additional operators. Up to the present we have considered only addition and subtraction operators. We will now augment this list by prefix plus and prefix minus. Examples of the use of prefix plus and minus are

$$+7 \qquad \text{prefix``+''}$$
$$-(4 + 6) \qquad \text{prefix``-,'' infix``+''}$$
$$4 + (-6) \qquad \text{infix``+,'' prefix``-''}$$

The prefix operators apply to a single operand. In the first case that operand is 7, in the second it is (4 + 6), and in the last it is 6. Therefore we could think of a prefixed operand as contrasted to a simple operand. This concept is brought out in the following syntax.

$$\langle \text{expression} \rangle :: = \langle \text{operand} \rangle \int [\langle \text{operator} \rangle \langle \text{operand} \rangle]$$
$$\langle \text{operator} \rangle :: = '+'|'-'$$
$$\langle \text{operand} \rangle :: = \langle \text{prefixed} \rangle | \langle \text{simple} \rangle$$
$$\langle \text{prefixed} \rangle :: = +\langle \text{simple} \rangle | -\langle \text{simple} \rangle$$
$$\langle \text{simple} \rangle :: = \langle \text{symbol} \rangle | \langle \text{constant} \rangle | \langle \text{subexpression} \rangle$$
$$\langle \text{subexpression} \rangle :: = (\langle \text{expression} \rangle)$$

It seems there is little to gain conceptually by looking at the corresponding computer algorithm that checks for proper expression syntax. Let us instead look at expressions from a different light.

5.4. Expression Conversion to Polish Form

In the previous discussion we considered syntax equations for describing various simplified forms of arithmetic expressions. We also examined computing algorithms for checking the validity of such expressions. We have not at this point broken down or translated an expression. The real goal of syntax directed expression processing is to break an expression down and convert it to some internal form (in this case we will convert to Polish form). This will be the topic of our present discussion.

We wish to develop a computing algorithm that will accept an expression from an input character string and produce a Polish form of that expression in an output string, as shown in Fig. 5.1.

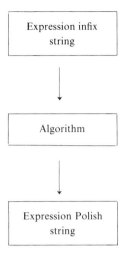

Figure 5.1.

For the infix side of the algorithm we already have a COMPARE operation that will test characters in the input stream and advance an INPUT CURSOR in case of a match. To create output an OUTPUT operation is required; OUTPUT (character) will output the specified character. When no character is declared, OUTPUT outputs the last character entered from the input stream.

To simplify the discussion of expression output we will only consider single character constants and symbols. A numeric character will be treated as a constant, an alpha character as a symbol. Thus a constant routine could be written to accept a constant from the input string and place that constant in the output string as follows.

```
CONSTANT:   CALL NUMERIC
            IF INDICATOR = 'TRUE' THEN OUTPUT
            RETURN
NUMERIC:    IF COMPARE '0' THEN INDICATOR = 'TRUE',
               RETURN
                 .
                 .
                 .
            IF COMPARE '9' THEN INDICATOR = 'TRUE',
               RETURN
            INDICATOR = 'FALSE', RETURN
```

A symbol routine would be formulated similarly.

```
SYMBOL:  CALL ALPHA
         IF INDICATOR = 'TRUE' THEN OUTPUT
         RETURN
ALPHA:   IF COMPARE 'A' THEN INDICATOR = 'TRUE', RETURN
              :
              :
         IF COMPARE 'Z' THEN INDICATOR = 'TRUE', RETURN
         INDICATOR = 'FALSE', RETURN
```

5.4.1. Syntax Considerations

Now let us look back to our first expression syntax for addition and subtraction operations. The syntax is

$$\langle expression \rangle :: = \langle operand \rangle \int [\,\langle operator \rangle \langle operand \rangle \,]$$
$$\langle operator \rangle :: = +\mid -$$
$$\langle operand \rangle :: = \langle constant \rangle \mid \langle symbol \rangle$$
$$\langle constant \rangle :: = \langle numeric \rangle$$
$$\langle symbol \rangle :: = \langle Alpha \rangle$$

This syntax supports expressions such as $4 + Y - 2$ or $7 - 3 - 4 + X + Y$. The syntax dictates the order of constants, symbols, and operators in an expression infix string.

A basic difference between infix and Polish forms is that infix operators appear between their operands rather than after them.

Infix: operand, operator, operand $(3, +, 4)$
Polish: operand, operand, operator $(3, 4, +)$

A syntax could be formed to prescribe this transposition when translating infix strings to Polish strings. The syntax would specify the order items are input from the infix string as well as the order items are output to the Polish string.

Input	Operations order	Output
3	accept operand	
	output operand	3
+	accept operator	
4	accept operand	
	output operand	4
	output operator	+

We will expand the syntax structure to support ordering operations. This will be done by showing subroutine calls in the syntax equations. These calls will be designated as underlined items, for example, OUTPUT(+). Now the syntax for infix to Polish ordering transformation appears as follows.

⟨expression⟩ :: = ⟨operand⟩∫ [+⟨operand⟩ output(+) | −⟨operand⟩ output(−)]
⟨operand⟩ :: = ⟨constant⟩ | ⟨symbol⟩
⟨constant⟩ :: = ⟨numeric⟩ output
⟨symbol⟩ :: = ⟨alpha⟩ output

This syntax dictates that all operands are to be output as they are encountered in the infix string. An operator, however, is not to be output until after its second operand.

5.4.2. Infix to Polish Algorithm

The algorithm for converting an infix string to Polish now follows directly from the expanded syntax. The syntax structure is simply imbedded into the statements of the algorithm.

(i1)		CALL EXPRESSION
(i2)		IF INDICATOR = 'FALSE' THEN HALT (IMPROPER INFIX)
(i3)		HALT (POLISH TRANSFORMATION COMPLETE)
(1)	EXPRESSION:	CALL OPERAND
(2)		IF INDICATOR = 'FALSE' THEN RETURN
(3)	EXPRESSION1:	IF NO COMPARE ' +' THEN GO TO EXPRESSION2
(4)		CALL OPERAND
(5)		IF INDICATOR = 'FALSE' THEN RETURN
(6)		OUTPUT (+)
(7)		GO TO EXPRESSION1
(8)	EXPRESSION2:	IF NO COMPARE ' −' THEN INDICATOR = 'TRUE', RETURN
(9)		CALL OPERAND
(10)		IF INDICATOR = 'FALSE' THEN RETURN
(11)		OUTPUT (−)
(12)		GO TO EXPRESSION1

```
(13) OPERAND:     CALL CONSTANT
(14)              IF INDICATOR = 'TRUE' THEN RETURN
(15)              CALL SYMBOL
(16)              RETURN
(17) CONSTANT:    CALL NUMERIC
(18)              IF INDICATOR = 'FALSE' THEN RETURN
(19)              OUTPUT
(20)              RETURN
(21) SYMBOL:      CALL ALPHA
(22)              IF INDICATOR = 'FALSE' THEN RETURN
(23)              OUTPUT
(24)              RETURN
```

This algorithm then processes all simple expressions formed from addition and subtraction operations. Examples of such expressions are.

$$X + 2$$
$$Y + 7 - 3$$
$$X + Y + Z - 2$$

The infix form of the expression is acted upon by the algorithm to produce a Polish string. In tracing the algorithm through an infix to Polish transformation we will keep track of four things.

(1) Return stack: Maintains a list of subroutine return addresses.
(2) Input cursor: Keeps the current position in the input infix string.
(3) Indicator: Designates the success or failure of processing through the syntax structure.
(4) Output: Forms the resultant Polish string.

The sample expression to be traced is

Position	Expression
1	X
2	+
3	7
4	−
5	3

Processing begins with the call to EXPRESSION at statement i1.

Statement executed	Action	Output	INPUT CURSOR	INDICATOR	Return stack
(i1)	Call expression		1		i1
(1)	Call operand				i1, 1
(13)	Call constant				i1, 1, 13
(17)	Constant not found at position 1			FALSE	
(18)	Return to statement 13 ·				i1, 1
(14)	No action				
(15)	Call symbol				i1, 1, 15
(21)	Symbol (X) found at position 1		2	TRUE	
(22)	No action				
(23)	Output symbol	X			
(24)	Return to statement 15				i1, 1
(16)	Return to statement 1				i1
(2)	No action				
(3)	Operator (+) found at position 2		3		
(4)	Call operand				i1, 4
(13)	Call constant				i1, 4, 13
(17)	Constant (7) found at position 3		4	TRUE	
(18)	No action				
(19)	Output constant	7			
(20)	Return to statement 13				i1, 4
(14)	Return to statement 4				i1
(5)	No action				
(6)	Output ' + '	+			
(7)	GO TO expression1				
(3)	Go to expression2				
(8)	Operator (−) found at position 4		5		
(9)	Call operand				i1, 9
(13)	Call constant				i1, 9, 13
(17)	Constant (3) found at position 5		6	TRUE	
(18)	No action				
(19)	Output constant	3			
(20)	Return to statement 13				i1, 9
(14)	Return to statement 9				i1
(10)	No action				
(11)	Output ' − '	−			
(12)	Go to expression1				
(3)	Go to expression2				
(8)	Return to statement i1			TRUE	empty
(i2)	No action				
(i3)	Halt (infix to Polish conversion complete)				

This completes the trace of the transformation of X + 7 − 3 to Polish form. Looking at the order of items output from the algorithm we see the string X, 7, +, 3, − was created. This string is, in fact, the desired Polish form.

5.4.3. Parenthetical Expressions

To process parenthetical expressions the syntax structure of our transformation algorithm must be expanded. The syntactical form of this expansion is already familiar to us. The operand syntax ⟨operand⟩ :: = ⟨constant⟩ | ⟨symbol⟩ must be expanded to accommodate subexpressions ⟨operand⟩ :: = ⟨constant⟩ | ⟨symbol⟩ | ⟨subexpression⟩, where ⟨subexpression⟩ :: = (⟨expression⟩). The resulting full syntax appears as follows.

⟨expression⟩:: = ⟨operand⟩∫[+⟨operand⟩ output(+)| − ⟨operand⟩ output(−)]
⟨operand⟩ :: = ⟨constant⟩|⟨symbol⟩|⟨subexpression⟩
⟨constant⟩::= ⟨numeric⟩⟨output⟩
⟨symbol⟩ :: = ⟨alpha⟩⟨output⟩
⟨subexpression⟩:: = (⟨expression⟩)

An algorithm formed from this syntax structure would transform simple parenthetical expressions into Polish form. Examples of such expressions are

$$X − (2 + Y)$$
$$X + (Z − 6)$$
$$Y + (2 − (X + 4))$$

This algorithm itself follows directly from the syntax equations. It is quite similar to the previous algorithm for which we traced the transformation of X + 7 − 3. For those of you who wish to know the exact changes from the previous algorithm they are as follows. Replace statement 16 of the OPERAND routine with the following three statements.

```
IF INDICATOR = 'TRUE' THEN RETURN
CALL SUBEXPRESSION
RETURN
```

Then add the SUBEXPRESSION routine to the end of the algorithm.

SUBEXPRESSION: IF NO COMPARE '(' THEN INDICATOR =
                 'FALSE', RETURN
                 CALL EXPRESSION
                 IF INDICATOR = 'FALSE' THEN RETURN
                 IF NO COMPARE ')' THEN INDICATOR =
                 'FALSE', RETURN
                 INDICATOR = 'TRUE', RETURN

This algorithm now treats a subexpression as an operand. We can observe that this effects proper infix to Polish conversion by recalling the order of transposition.

Infix		Polish	
operand	X	operand	X
operator	−	operand	7
operand	7	operator	−

In a parenthetical expression such as $X - (7 + Y)$ the entire subexpression $(7 + Y)$ is treated as an operand. The resulting transposition is then

Infix		Polish	
operand	X	operand	X
operator	−	operand	$(7 + Y)$
operand	$(7 + Y)$	operator	−

Now the subexpression $(7 + Y)$ is treated as an expression in itself and transformed to Polish $7, Y, +$. Substituting the subexpression Polish form into the above we have

Infix	Polish
$X - (7 + Y)$	$X, 7, Y + -$

As you can see, the algorithm will make the proper transformation of a parenthetical expression into Polish form.

5.4.4. Addition of Operators

In the previous transformation algorithms we considered only ex-pressions formed with addition and subtraction operators. As more operators are supported, the order priority of operator application will have to be considered. The fact that addition and subtraction are of the same priority simplified our earlier algorithms. Equal priority operators are applied in a consistent left-to-right (in our example top to bottom) order. As a result, when converting to Polish we simply transposed the operator with its second operand. For example:

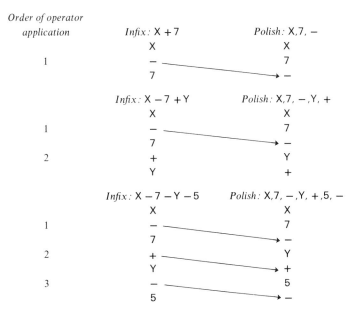

Then we considered the use of parentheses in forming an expression. Here we noticed that parenthetical subexpressions altered the order of operator application, and therefore the transposition of operators and operands when converting to Polish. For example:

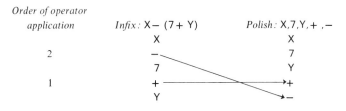

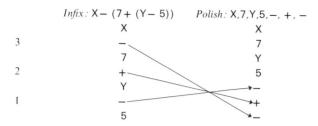

When considering additional operators, their priorities will dictate a natural alteration in the order of operator application. For example, the priority 1 multiplication "*" and division "/" operators are naturally applied before the priority 2 addition " + " and subtraction " − " operators. For example:

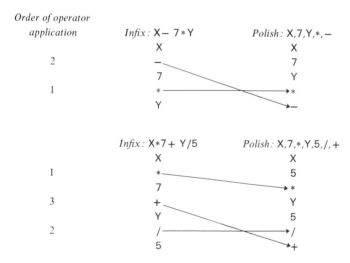

It is the duty of the syntax structure in our algorithm to perform the proper conversion transposition. Imbedded in the syntax is the order in which items are accepted from the infix string and the order in which items are output to the Polish string.

You may have noted in the previous examples that operators are positioned in the Polish string in the order in which they are to be applied.[1]

---

[1] The reader may wish to note that operators are not necessarily applied in the precise order dictated by operator priority. For example, in expression $X + Y − Z*2$ the higher priority of the "*" operator dictates that it be applied first. However the " + " operator could be applied first, then the "*," and finally the " − ." In fact, this will be the order of application we will use for similar expressions.

For example, in the Polish form of X − 7∗Y the "∗" is positioned before the " −," and in the expression X − (7 + Y) the " +" before the " −," but in expression X − 7 + Y the " −" is positioned before the " +."

The syntax must detect the order of application and position operators in the Polish string accordingly. With " +," " −," "∗," and "/" operators the "∗" and "/" operators are applied before the " +" and " −" operators. The syntax equations must specify an ordering that holds back " +" and " −" operators from the Polish output while scanning for "/" and "∗" operators. On occurrence of the next " +" or " −" operator the "held" operator may then be output. This ordering is supported by the following syntax.

$$\langle \text{expression} \rangle ::= \langle \text{priority1} \rangle \int [\; + \; \langle \text{priority1} \rangle \; \underline{\text{output}(+)} \; | $$
$$\qquad\qquad - \; \langle \text{priority1} \rangle \; \underline{\text{output}(-)} \;]$$
$$\langle \text{priority1} \rangle ::= \langle \text{operand} \rangle \int [\; * \; \langle \text{operand} \rangle \; \underline{\text{output}(*)} \; | $$
$$\qquad\qquad / \; \langle \text{operand} \rangle \; \underline{\text{output}(/)} \;]$$
$$\langle \text{operand} \rangle ::= \langle \text{constant} \rangle \; | \; \langle \text{symbol} \rangle \; | \; \langle \text{subexpression} \rangle$$
$$\langle \text{subexpression} \rangle ::= (\; \langle \text{expression} \rangle \;)$$

Note that when a " +" or " −" operator is detected in the first equation, PRIORITY 1 is called before OUTPUT (+) or OUTPUT (−). From PRIORITY 1 the higher priority "/" and "∗" operators are output. This ordering satisfies our requirement for the position of operators in the Polish string.

The ordering is effected in a computing algorithm by imbedding the syntax structure into the statements of the algorithm. This algorithm appears as follows.

(i1)		CALL EXPRESSION
(i2)		IF INDICATOR = 'FALSE' THEN HALT (IMPROPER INFIX STRING)
(i3)		HALT (POLISH TRANSFORMATION COMPLETE)
(1)	EXPRESSION:	CALL PRIORITY 1 IF INDICATOR = 'FALSE' THEN RETURN
(3)	EXPRESSION1:	IF NO COMPARE '+' THEN GO TO EXPRESSION2
(4)		CALL PRIORITY1
(5)		IF INDICATOR = 'FALSE' THEN RETURN
(6)		OUTPUT(+)
(7)		RETURN
(8)	EXPRESSION2:	IF NO COMPARE '−' THEN INDICATOR = 'TRUE', RETURN

(9)		CALL PRIORITY1
(10)		IF INDICATOR = 'FALSE' THEN RETURN
(11)		OUTPUT(−)
(12)		RETURN
(13)	PRIORITY I:	CALL OPERAND
(14)		IF INDICATOR = 'FALSE' THEN RETURN
(15)	PRIORITY I1:	IF NO COMPARE '∗' THEN GO TO PRIORITY I2
(16)		CALL OPERAND
(17)		IF INDICATOR = 'FALSE' THEN RETURN
(18)		OUTPUT(∗)
(19)		RETURN
(20)	PRIORITY I2:	IF NO COMPARE '/' THEN INDICATOR = 'TRUE', RETURN
(21)		CALL OPERAND
(22)		IF INDICATOR = 'FALSE' THEN RETURN
(23)		OUTPUT(/)
(24)		RETURN
(25)	OPERAND:	CALL CONSTANT
(26)		IF INDICATOR = 'TRUE' THEN RETURN
(27)		CALL SYMBOL
(28)		IF INDICATOR = 'TRUE' THEN RETURN
(29)		CALL SUBEXPRESSION
(30)		RETURN
(31)	SUBEXPRESSION:	IF NO COMPARE 'C' THEN INDICATOR = 'FALSE', RETURN
(32)		CALL EXPRESSION
(33)		IF INDICATOR = 'FALSE' THEN RETURN
(34)		IF NO COMPARE ')' THEN INDICATOR = 'FALSE', RETURN
(35)		INDICATOR = 'TRUE'
(36)		RETURN

Let us trace $X - 7*Y$ through the algorithm. In the trace we will see how the " + " operator is held until after the "∗" operator is output, resulting in the Polish string $X,7,Y,*,-$.

Position	Expression
1	X
2	−
3	7
4	∗
5	Y

We will begin tracing the expression with statement i1. Operations in the trace are shown by the output, INPUT CURSOR, INDICATOR, and return stack.

Statement executed	Action	Output	INPUT CURSOR	INDICATOR	Return stack
(i1)	Call expression		1		i1
(1)	Call expression				i1, 1
(13)	Call operand				i1, 1, 13
(25)	Constant not found at position 1			FALSE	
(26)	No action				
(27)	Symbol (X) found at position 1	X	2	TRUE	
(28)	Return to statement 13				i1, 1
(14)	No action				
(15)	Go to priority12				
(20)	Return to statement 1			TRUE	i1
(2)	No action				
(3)	Go to expression2				
(8)	Operator (−) found at position 2		3		
(9)	Call priority1				i1, 9
(13)	Call operand				i1, 9, 13
(25)	Constant (7) found at position 3	7	4	TRUE	
(26)	Return to statement 13				i1, 9
(14)	No action				
(15)	Operator (∗) found at position 4		5		
(16)	Call operand				i1, 9, 16
(25)	No constant found at position 5			FALSE	
(26)	No action				
(27)	Symbol (Y) found at position 5	Y	6	TRUE	
(28)	Return to statement 16				i1, 19
(17)	No action				
(18)	Output "∗"	∗			
(19)	Return to statement 9				i1
(10)	No action				
(11)	Output " − "	−			
(12)	Return to statement i1				empty
(i2)	No action				
(i3)	Halt (Polish transformation complete)				

The items output from our algorithm were X,7,Y,∗,−. This in fact is the proper Polish string for X − 7∗Y.

Let us now return to the subject of adding operators. Presently we support " + " and " − " operators, as well as the higher priority "∗" and "/" operators. We can now add the exponentiation (↑) operator. It will take the highest priority of all.

$$
\begin{aligned}
&\text{Priority 1:} && \uparrow \\
&\text{Priority 2:} && *,/ \\
&\text{Priority 3:} && +, -
\end{aligned}
$$

The addition of a third priority to the expression structure imposes another ordering requirement on the syntax. As before, the " + " and " − " operators must be held back until "∗" and "/" operators are processed. Now, furthermore, the "∗" and "/" operators must be held back until the " ↑ " operator is processed. This is reflected in the syntax equations as follows.

⟨expression⟩ :: = ⟨priority 2⟩ ∫ [+ ⟨priority 2⟩ <u>output(+)</u> |
                                            − ⟨priority 2⟩ <u>output(−)</u>]
⟨priority 2⟩ :: = ⟨priority 1⟩ ∫ [∗ ⟨priority 1⟩ <u>output(∗)</u> |
                                        / ⟨priority 1⟩ <u>output(/)</u>]
⟨priority 1⟩ :: = ⟨operand⟩ ∫ [↑ ⟨operand⟩ <u>output(↑)</u>]
⟨operand⟩ :: = ⟨constant⟩ | ⟨symbol⟩ | ⟨subexpression⟩
⟨subexpression⟩ :: = (⟨expression⟩)

In the first equation, when a priority 3 " + " or " − " operator is detected, a call is made to process PRIORITY 2 operators before the priority 3 operator is output. In the second equation priority 2 operators of "∗" and "/" call for the processing of PRIORITY 1 operators before the priority 2 operator is output. This syntax dictates the proper order for creating a Polish string.

We could, as before, create an algorithm that incorporates this syntax structure. The algorithm would then process parenthetical expressions over a three-priority operator structure. However, the algorithm follows in a reasonable, straightforward manner from the syntax. Instead of formulating this algorithm, we will go on to somewhat different considerations.

5.5. Coded Format

We are now able to build an algorithm that accepts an infix string as input, parses the expression, and produces a Polish string as output. Let us stop for a moment and consider the purpose of creating Polish forms. The parsing and transformation of expressions is not a goal in itself. It is simply a means for formatting the input to an assembler, compiler, or information retrieval or other language processing system. The system demands a convenient format for internal processing.

Certainly the conversion of infix to Polish provides a convenience in itself. But the parsing algorithm could go a step further. Each operator, symbol, and constant in the Polish string could be coded for easy identification by the language processing system. In the process of transforming an expression to Polish form the parsing algorithm must identify each item of the expression. Given the identification of an item, it is a simple matter to output a code for that item rather than the item itself.

Let us consider the following coding scheme for symbols, constants and operators.

> symbol: code 1, symbol string
> constant: code 2, constant value
> +operator: code 3
> −operator: code 4
> *operator: code 5
> /operator: code 6
> ↑operator: code 7

With this scheme the coded Polish form of X, +, 7, *, Y would appear as follows.

> code 1, X
> code 2, 7
> code 1, Y
> code 5
> code 3

However, in the following discussion, we will not consider specific code values. Instead of "code 5" we will talk about "multiplication code"; instead of "code 3" we will use "addition code."

You will notice we did not mention "prefix minus code" or "prefix plus code." Actually these operators will not exist in the Polish string. When a prefix plus is encountered in the infix string it will simply be ignored; it has no effect on the value of the expression anyway. On the other hand, a minus will be transformed to a subtraction operation. For example

(− 7) will be treated as though it were written 0 − 7; − (X ↑ 2 + 3) as 0 − (X ↑ 2 + 3). The syntax will indicate that a zero is forced into the output string in front of the operand to prefix minus, and a subtraction operator after the operand.

A syntax will be created to support the following infix operators.

Priority 1: prefix plus, prefix minus
Priority 2: exponentiation
Priority 3: multiplication, division
Priority 4: addition, subtraction

This syntax will show the structure for an algorithm to transform infix expressions to coded Polish form.

⟨expression⟩ :: = ⟨priority 3⟩ ∫ [+ ⟨priority 3⟩ output (addition code)|
                                − ⟨priority 3⟩ output (subtraction code)]
⟨priority 3⟩ :: = ⟨priority 2⟩ ∫ [* ⟨priority 2⟩ output (multiplication code) |
                             / ⟨priority 2⟩ output (division code)
⟨priority 2⟩ :: = ⟨priority 1⟩ ∫ [↑ ⟨priority 1⟩ output (exponentiation code)]
⟨priority 1⟩ :: = − ⟨output '0 constant'⟩ ⟨operand⟩ output (subtraction code) |
                      + ⟨operand⟩ | ⟨operand⟩
⟨operand⟩ :: = ⟨constant⟩ | ⟨symbol⟩ | ⟨subexpression⟩
⟨subexpression⟩ :: = (⟨expression⟩)

An algorithm based on this syntax structure would handle the complete preprocessing of an arithmetic expression. The expression would be checked for validity and transformed into a Polish string. The basic elements (operators, symbols, and constants) of the string would be presented in coded form. In short, the expression would be presented in a most convenient form to the language processing system. The algorithm for doing this appears as follows.

```
              CALL EXPRESSION
              IF INDICATOR = 'FALSE' THEN HALT
                 (IMPROPER INFIX)
              HALT (CODED POLISH TRANSFORMATION
              COMPLETE)
EXPRESSION:   CALL PRIORITY3
              IF INDICATOR = 'FALSE' THEN RETURN
```

```
EXPRESSION1:      IF NO COMPARE '+' THEN GO TO EXPRESSION2
                  CALL PRIORITY3
                  IF INDICATOR = 'FALSE' THEN RETURN
                  OUTPUT (ADDITION CODE)
                  GO TO EXPRESSION1
EXPRESSION2:      IF NO COMPARE '-' THEN INDICATOR = 'TRUE',
                     RETURN
                  CALL PRIORITY3
                  IF INDICATOR = 'FALSE' THEN RETURN
                  OUTPUT (SUBTRACTION CODE)
                  GO TO EXPRESSION1
PRIORITY3:        CALL PRIORITY2
                  IF INDICATOR = 'FALSE' THEN RETURN
PRIORITY31:       IF NO COMPARE '*' THEN GO TO PRIORITY32
                  CALL PRIORITY2
                  IF INDICATOR = 'FALSE' THEN RETURN
                  OUTPUT (MULTIPLICATION CODE)
                  GO TO PRIORITY31
PRIORITY32:       IF NO COMPARE '/' THEN INDICATOR ← 'TRUE',
                     RETURN
                  CALL PRIORITY2
                  IF INDICATOR = 'FALSE' THEN RETURN
                  OUTPUT (DIVISION CODE)
                  GO TO PRIORITY31
PRIORITY2:        CALL PRIORITY1
                  IF INDICATOR = 'FALSE' THEN RETURN
PRIORITY21:       IF NO COMPARE '↑' THEN INDICATOR ← 'TRUE',
                     RETURN
                  CALL PRIORITY1
                  IF INDICATOR = 'FALSE' THEN RETURN
                  OUTPUT (EXPONENTIATION CODE)
                  GO TO PRIORITY21
PRIORITY1:        IF NO COMPARE '-' THEN GO TO PRIORITY11
                  OUTPUT (0 CONSTANT)
                  CALL OPERAND
                  IF INDICATOR = 'FALSE' THEN RETURN
                  OUTPUT (SUBTRACTION CODE)
                     RETURN
PRIORITY11:       IF NO COMPARE '+' THEN GO TO PRIORITY12
PRIORITY12:       CALL OPERAND
                     RETURN
```

OPERAND: CALL CONSTANT
                     IF INDICATOR = 'FALSE' THEN GO TO OPERAND1
                     RETURN
OPERAND1:   CALL SYMBOL
                     IF INDICATOR = 'FALSE' THEN GO TO OPERAND2
                     RETURN
OPERAND2:   CALL SUBEXPRESSION
                     RETURN
SUBEXPRESSION: IF NO COMPARE '(' THEN INDICATOR = 'FALSE',
                     RETURN
                     CALL EXPRESSION
                     IF INDICATOR = 'FALSE' THEN RETURN
                     IF NO COMPARE '(' THEN INDICATOR = 'FALSE',
                     RETURN

We will defer the processing of this algorithm to the next chapter. There, methods will be considered for processing an expression structure directly from the syntax equations. At this time we will go on to describe the syntax and parsing of complete commands.

5.6. Coding a Complete Language

Up to this point we have built a process for converting programmed expressions to coded form. We will now extend this process to a complete programming language.

The language will be a subset of a scientific compiler. It will include two executable commands: ASSIGNMENT and GO TO. Examples of each are

Assignment commands
X = 5*Y +3
Z = (X +Y)*5
⟨assignment⟩ :: = ⟨variable⟩ = ⟨expression⟩

Go to commands
GO TO LABEL1
GO TO LABEL2
⟨go to⟩ :: = GO TO ⟨label⟩

The go to command references labels on other commands. A label is declared for a command by prefixing the command with a label name followed by a colon. For example:

Label commands
LABEL1: X = 5*Y + 3
LABEL2: GO TO LABEL1
⟨labeled command⟩ :: = ⟨label⟩ : ⟨command⟩

Our compiler will also support two nonexecutable statements: DECLARE and SUBROUTINE. Examples of these are

Declare statements
DECLARE X(FLOATING) Y(FIXED)
DECLARE Z(FIXED)
⟨declare⟩ :: = DECLARE ∫[⟨variable⟩ (⟨attribute⟩)]
⟨attribute⟩ :: = FLOATING | FIXED

Subroutine statements
SUBROUTINE SQRT(N)
SUBROUTINE MAX(X, Y)
⟨subroutine⟩ :: = SUBROUTINE ⟨subroutine name⟩ (variable ∫[, ⟨variable⟩])

A program is built from a set of nonexecutable statements followed by a set of executable commands and terminated by an END statement. We can then declare the legal forms of a program by syntax equations. The following is our program syntax.

⟨program⟩ :: = ∫[⟨nonexecutable statement⟩]
            ∫[⟨executable statement⟩] ⟨end⟩
⟨nonexecutable statement⟩ :: = ⟨declare⟩ | ⟨subroutine⟩
⟨executable statement⟩ :: = ⟨label⟩ : ⟨command⟩ | ⟨command⟩
⟨command⟩ :: = ⟨assignment⟩ | ⟨go to⟩
⟨declare⟩ :: = DECLARE ∫[⟨variable⟩ (⟨attribute⟩)]
⟨attribute⟩ :: = FIXED | FLOATING
⟨subroutine⟩ :: = SUBROUTINE ⟨subroutine name⟩ (⟨variable⟩ ∫[, ⟨variable⟩])
⟨go to⟩ :: = GO TO ⟨label⟩
⟨assignment⟩ :: = ⟨variable⟩ = ⟨expression⟩
⟨end⟩ :: = END
⟨expression⟩ :: = ...

Now the goal of this section is to create a process converting such a program to coded form. For this process we will associate a unique code value with each type of statement. These codes will be

Statement type	Code
⟨declare⟩	1
⟨subroutine⟩	2
⟨go to⟩	3
⟨assignment⟩	4
⟨end⟩	5

We already have a process for coding arithmetic expressions in a program. What we are after now is a process for coding the programmed statements. For this process we can create a conversion syntax that declares those codes to which each statement is converted. This syntax appears as follows.

⟨program⟩ :: = ∫ [⟨nonexecutable statement⟩]
           ∫ [⟨executable statement⟩] ⟨end⟩
⟨nonexecutable statement⟩ :: = ⟨declare⟩ | ⟨subroutine⟩
⟨executable statement⟩ :: = ⟨label⟩ : ⟨command⟩ | ⟨command⟩
⟨command⟩ :: = ⟨assignment⟩ | ⟨go to⟩
⟨declare⟩ :: = DECLARE output(1) ∫ [⟨variable⟩ (⟨attribute⟩)]
⟨attribute⟩ :: = FIXED | FLOATING
⟨subroutine⟩ :: = SUBROUTINE output(2) ⟨subroutine name⟩
           (⟨variable⟩ ∫ [, ⟨variable⟩])
⟨go to⟩ :: = GO TO output(3) ⟨label⟩
⟨assignment⟩ :: = output(4) ⟨variable⟩ = ⟨expression⟩
⟨end⟩ :: = END output(5)
⟨expression⟩ :: = . . .

Now an algorithm based on this syntax can be formulated. For this algorithm our familiar CALL, RETURN, COMPARE, and OUTPUT operations will be used. The algorithm accepts a program as input and produces a coded form of that program as output. The following is our conversion algorithm.

PROGRAM: CALL NONEXECUTABLE
           IF INDICATOR = 'TRUE' THEN GO TO PROGRAM

```
PROGRAM1:     CALL EXECUTABLE
              IF INDICATOR = 'TRUE' THEN GO TO PROGRAM1
              CALL END
              IF INDICATOR = 'FALSE' THEN HALT
              (IMPROPER PROGRAM)
              HALT (PROGRAM CONVERSION COMPLETE)
NONEXECUTABLE:  CALL DECLARE
              IF INDICATOR = 'TRUE' THEN RETURN
              CALL SUBROUTINE
              RETURN
EXECUTABLE:   CALL LABEL
              IF INDICATOR = 'FALSE' THEN GO TO
              EXECUTABLE1
              IF NO COMPARE ':' THEN INDICATOR = 'FALSE',
              RETURN
EXECUTABLE1:  CALL COMMAND
              RETURN
COMMAND:      CALL ASSIGNMENT
              IF INDICATOR = 'TRUE' THEN RETURN
              CALL GOTO
DECLARE:      CALL VARIABLE
              IF INDICATOR = 'FALSE' THEN INDICATOR =
              'TRUE', RETURN
              IF NO COMPARE '(' THEN INDICATOR = 'FALSE',
              RETURN
              CALL ATTRIBUTE
              IF INDICATOR = 'FALSE' THEN RETURN
              IF NO COMPARE '(' THEN INDICATOR = 'FALSE'
              RETURN
              GO TO DECLARE1
ATTRIBUTE:    IF COMPARE 'FIXED' THEN INDICATOR = 'TRUE',
              RETURN
              IF COMPARE 'FLOATING' THEN INDICATOR =
              'TRUE', RETURN
              INDICATOR = 'FALSE'
              RETURN
SUBROUTINE:   IF NO COMPARE 'SUBROUTINE' THEN
              INDICATOR = 'FALSE', RETURN
              OUTPUT (CODE2)
              CALL SUBROUTINE NAME
              IF INDICATOR = 'FALSE' THEN RETURN
```

```
                    IF NO COMPARE '(' THEN INDICATOR = 'FALSE',
                       RETURN
SUBROUTINE1:        CALL VARIABLE
                    IF INDICATOR = 'FALSE' THEN RETURN
                    IF COMPARE '(' THEN GO TO SUBROUTINE1
                    IF NO COMPARE '(' THEN INDICATOR = 'FALSE',
                       RETURN
                    RETURN
          GOTO:     IF NO COMPARE 'GO' THEN INDICATOR =
                       'FALSE', RETURN
                    IF NO COMPARE 'TO' THEN INDICATOR =
                       'TRUE', RETURN
                    OUTPUT (CODE3)
                    CALL LABEL
                    RETURN
ASSIGNMENT:         OUTPUT (CODE4)
                    CALL VARIABLE
                    IF INDICATOR = 'FALSE' THEN RETURN
                    IF NO COMPARE '=' THEN INDICATOR = 'FALSE',
                       RETURN
                    CALL EXPRESSION
                    RETURN
          END:      IF NO COMPARE 'END' THEN INDICATOR =
                       'FALSE', RETURN
                    OUTPUT(CODE5)
                    INDICATOR = 'TRUE'
                    RETURN
EXPRESSION:         (previous expression conversion algorithm)
```

5.7. Summary

In processing a programming language it is sometimes helpful to reduce the language to a coded form. A process for performing this reduction can be based on syntax equations. The equations specify the code values for each segment of the language. An algorithm, structured on this syntax, can then be formulated to perform coded reduction of the programming language.

5.8
exercises

(1) Write syntax equations for a symbol with the following characteristics.
   (a) Five to ten characters in length
   (b) First two characters alpha
   (c) Next three characters numeric
   (d) Remaining characters alphanumeric

(2) Form syntax equations for converting standard form Boolean expressions to Polish form. Support equal priority AND and OR operators in this syntax.

(3) Form a compiler-like algorithm based on the syntax in Question 2.

(4) Alter syntax equations on page 73 to support the following standard form operator priorities.

Priority	Operator
1	" + " and " − "
2	↑
3	"/" and "*"

(5) Alter the syntax equations on page 73 to support the encoding of an expression in standard form rather than Polish form.

6
syntax driven
algorithms

Up to this point we have considered syntax directed parsing algorithms. The structure of the algorithm was directed by a set of syntax equations. This was done by writing a parsing algorithm that incorporated the syntax structure in the algorithm commands. We will now take a further step and look at syntax driven parsing algorithms.

The syntax equations will be used directly in the parsing algorithm. They will be represented in tabular form. A syntax driver will then be used to step through these tabular forms. The driver will match the form of an incoming programming language to the forms presented in the syntax tables, in this way parsing the language.

6.1. Syntax Tables

Let us think in terms of a separate table for each syntax equation. Items in the table represent corresponding items in the syntax equation, and the table will be identified by the same name as the syntax equation. For example:

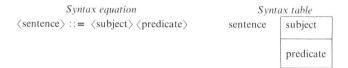

| | *Syntax equation* | | *Syntax table* | |

Syntax equation	*Syntax table*
⟨sentence⟩ ∷= ⟨subject⟩ ⟨predicate⟩	sentence

subject
predicate

Items in the table will be categorized according to the type of syntactical entity. For example, consider the categories in the following syntax tables.

Syntax equations   *Syntax tables*

⟨sentence⟩ ∷= ⟨subject⟩ ⟨predicate⟩   sentence

equation	subject
equation	predicate
end of table	

⟨article⟩ ∷= A | THE   article

literal	A
or	———
literal	THE
end of table	———

If you will recall, in a previous discussion (see Chapter 4) we formed a syntax for a subset of the English language. At this time we will convert that syntax to tabular form.

Syntax equations   *Tabular form*

⟨sentence⟩ ∷= ⟨subject⟩ ⟨predicate⟩   sentence

equation	subject
equation	predicate
end of table	

⟨subject⟩ ∷= ⟨noun phrase⟩   subject

equation	noun phrase
end of table	———

Syntax equations		*Tabular form*	

⟨predicate⟩ ::= ⟨verb⟩ ⟨object⟩   predicate

equation	verb
equation	object
end of table	———

⟨object⟩ ::= ⟨noun phrase⟩   object

equation	noun phrase
end of table	———

⟨noun phrase⟩ ::= ⟨article⟩ ⟨noun⟩   noun phrase

equation	article
equation	noun
end of table	———

⟨article⟩ ::= A | THE   article

literal	A
or	———
literal	THE
end of table	———

⟨noun⟩ ::= CAT | TREE   noun

literal	CAT
or	———
literal	THE
end of table	———

⟨verb⟩ ::= CLIMBS   verb

literal	CLIMBS
end of table	———

6.2. Syntax Driver

Now we will formulate a driver to step through these tables. The driver will try to match a sentence like "THE CAT CLIMBS A TREE" to the syntax tables. In doing this it must keep track of the current sentence position.

The sentence is held, internal to the computer, as a string of characters or words. An INPUT CURSOR is used by the driver to position itself in the sentence. When processing begins, the cursor will point to the first word of the sentence; INPUT CURSOR = 1. As processing continues the cursor is advanced into the sentence; when positioned at the ith word, INPUT CURSOR = i.

As the sentence is processed, sentence words are matched against items in the syntax tables. In doing this the driver will keep track of its current syntax table position as "SYNTAX POSITION." The syntax position is placed at the first item of a syntax table by assigning the table name. For example, with the above tables, if we assign ARTICLE to SYNTAX POSITION, then the current table item will be LITERAL(A).

To advance the syntax position within a table it is simply incremented. For example, after the above assignment, INCREMENT (SYNTAX POSITION) advances the position to the OR item of the ARTICLE syntax table.

The driver will keep the INPUT CURSOR and SYNTAX POSITION in a STACK. In fact, it will keep a series of cursors and positions. As the driver works its way down a series of syntax equations, it stacks the INPUT CURSOR and SYNTAX POSITION for each equation. Then, when the driver is ready to return back up through the equations, it has a memory of which equations to return to.

It also has, in the stack, a memory of INPUT CURSORS. In case the driver has taken a false path through the syntax equations it restores the INPUT CURSOR from the stack. The driver can then try an alternate path with the original INPUT CURSOR.

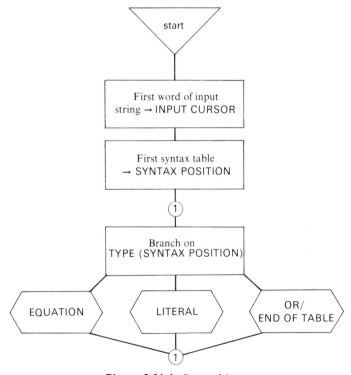

Figure 6.1(a). Syntax driver.

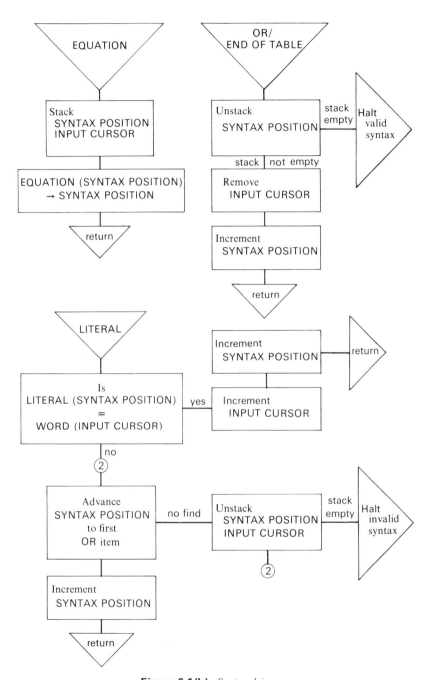

Figure 6.1(b). Syntax driver.

In contrast to our previous programmed parsing algorithms, a syntax driven algorithm does not have to maintain a TRUE/FALSE indicator. Since it operates directly on the syntax structure, a syntax driven algorithm can take TRUE and FALSE routes directly through the syntax. This is seen in Fig. 6.1, the flow chart of the syntax driver.

In this flow chart the familiar STACK and UNSTACK operations are used. In addition, an unfamiliar REMOVE operation is incorporated. The REMOVE (X) operation removes an item from the stack, but unlike the UNSTACK operation, it does not assign that item to X.

This algorithm will be translated into compiler-like computer code. We then have a standard computerized syntax driver. The driver can be applied to any problem in language processing by simply replacing the syntax tables.

```
(1)   START:    INPUT CURSOR = 1
(2)             SYNTAX POSITION = FIRST SYNTAX TABLE
(3)   LABEL1:   IF TYPE(SYNTAX POSITION) = 'EQUATION' THEN
(4)                STACK(SYNTAX POSITION)
(5)                STACK(INPUT CURSOR)
(6)                SYNTAX POSITION = EQUATION(SYNTAX POSITION)
(7)                GO TO LABEL1
(8)             END
(9)             IF TYPE(SYNTAX POSITION) = 'OR'|'END OF
                TABLE' THEN
(10)               IF STACK = EMPTY THEN HALT(VALID SYNTAX)
(11)               UNSTACK(SYNTAX POSITION)
(12)               REMOVE(INPUT CURSOR)
(13)               INCREMENT(SYNTAX POSITION)
(14)               GO TO LABEL1
(15)            END
(16)            IF TYPE(SYNTAX POSITION) = 'LITERAL' THEN
(17)               IF LITERAL(SYNTAX POSITION) = WORD(INPUT
                   CURSOR) THEN
(18)                  INCREMENT(INPUT CURSOR)
(19)                  INCREMENT(SYNTAX POSITION)
(20)                  GO TO LABEL1
(21)               END
(22)               IF LITERAL(SYNTAX POSITION) ≠ WORD(INPUT
                   CURSOR) THEN
(23)  LABEL2:        INCREMENT(SYNTAX POSITION)
(24)                  IF TYPE(SYNTAX POSITION) ≠ 'OR' | 'END OF
                      TABLE' THEN
```

(25)	GO TO LABEL2
(26)	END
(27)	IF TYPE(SYNTAX POSITION) = 'END OF TABLE' THEN
(28)	IF STACK = EMPTY THEN HALT(INVALID SYNTAX)
(29)	UNSTACK(SYNTAX POSITION)
(30)	UNSTACK(INPUT CURSOR)
(31)	GO TO LABEL2
(32)	END
(33)	IF TYPE(SYNTAX POSITION) = 'OR' THEN
(34)	INCREMENT(SYNTAX POSITION)
(35)	GO TO LABEL1
(36)	END
(37)	END
(38)	END

Let us now trace this algorithm through its first stages in parsing "THE CAT CLIMBS A TREE." It will begin with the assignment of INPUT CURSOR to the first word of the sentence (INPUT CURSOR = 1). As parsing progresses the INPUT CURSOR will be advanced into the sentence. The cursor positions of each word in the sentence are as follows.

Sentence word	Input cursor position
THE	1
CAT	2
CLIMBS	3
A	4
TREE	5

The syntax tables used will be those previously shown. The SYNTAX POSITION will point at these tables. The pointer will be specified by table name and item number in that table. For example, SYNTAX CURSOR = PREDICATE(2) points to the second item EQUATION(OBJECT) in the predicate syntax table.

The trace will show the operation performed by algorithm statement number. It appears as

(1)	1 → INPUT CURSOR
(2)	SENTENCE(1) → SYNTAX POSITION
(3)	SINCE TYPE(SENTENCE(1)) = EQUATION THEN
(4)	STACK(SENTENCE(1))

```
(5)    STACK(CURSOR = 1)
(6)    SUBJECT → SYNTAX POSITION
(7)    GO TO LABEL1
(3)    SINCE TYPE(SUBJECT(1)) = EQUATION THEN
(4)    STACK(SUBJECT(1))
(5)    STACK(CURSOR = 1)
(6)    NOUN PHRASE → SYNTAX POSITION
(7)    GO TO LABEL1
(3)    SINCE TYPE(NOUN PHRASE(1)) = EQUATION THEN
(4)    STACK(NOUN PHRASE(1))
(5)    STACK(CURSOR = 1)
(6)    ARTICLE(1) → SYNTAX POSITION
(7)    GO TO LABEL1
(16)   SINCE TYPE(ARTICLE(1)) = LITERAL THEN
(22)   SINCE WORD(1) ≠ A THEN
(23)   ARTICLE(2) → SYNTAX POSITION
(33)   SINCE TYPE(ARTICLE(2)) = OR THEN
(34)   ARTICLE(3) → SYNTAX POSITION
(35)   GO TO LABEL1
(16)   SINCE TYPE(ARTICLE(3)) = LITERAL THEN
(17)   SINCE WORD(1) = THE THEN
(18)   2 → INPUT CURSOR
        ·
        ·
        ·
```

6.3. Text Processing

As you may have noticed, in the parsing algorithm we have somewhat over-simplified the processing of incoming text. The sentence was treated as an incoming stream of words rather than as characters.

In actual practice a sentence would typically be represented in the computer as a string of characters. The driver would then test for LITERALS on a character-by-character basis. It would also scan blank characters between LITERALS.

6.4. Repeat Processing

To simplify the syntax structures we introduced a repeat operator. An example of this was the adjective list of a noun phrase, the syntax equation of which follows.

$$\langle noun\ phrase\rangle::=\langle article\rangle \int [\langle adjective\rangle]\langle noun\rangle$$

In the tabular form of syntax equations an additional type of table entry is used for repeat. The repeated items, accessed by the repeat entry, are then split off in a separate syntax table. This can be seen in the tabular form of the above syntax equation.

noun phrase	equation repeat equation end of table	article noun phrase 1 noun ————
noun phrase 1	equation end of table	adjective ————

A corresponding change will be made in the syntax driver. When the driver encounters a repeat entry in the syntax table, it iterates the application of the repeated syntax table. The driver, with this change, appears as shown in Fig. 6.2.

6.5. Coded Conversion Processing

We now have a syntax driver capable of checking the validity of a free-form incoming language. However, there is no facility in this driver for converting a language to coded form. In fact, there is no facility for any output whatsoever.

We will now expand the driver to support output. It will maintain an OUTPUT CURSOR. Output will be held in a character string, with the OUTPUT CURSOR designating the current string position. The OUTPUT CURSOR will be kept, together with INPUT CURSOR and SYNTAX POSITION, in the stack. In case a false path is taken through the syntax structure, the driver can then restore the OUTPUT CURSOR before trying an alternate path.

The driver will support a generalized programmed subroutine facility. The INPUT CURSOR and OUTPUT CURSOR are made available to a called subroutine. In this way the subroutine can process text from the input stream and/or output text to the output string. When a subroutine completes processing it returns to the driver with a TRUE or FALSE condition. In this way the subroutine indicates the validity of the current path charted through the syntax structure.

A particular example of a subroutine is the coding subroutine. OUTPUT(I) can be a general subroutine used to output code values to the output string. Since this subroutine only processes output text it can never detect an invalid condition in the input text; it will never return FALSE.

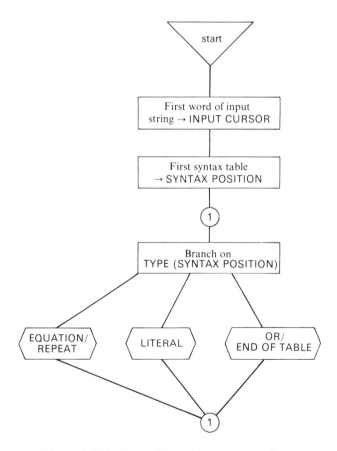

Figure 6.2(a). Syntax driver with repeat processing.

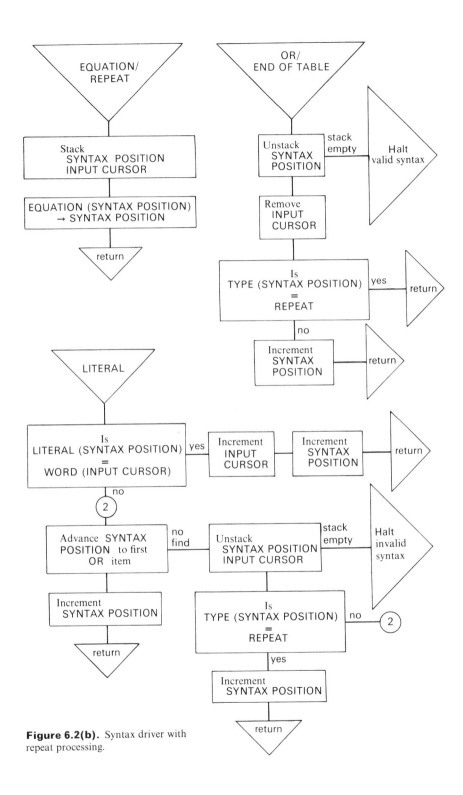

Figure 6.2(b). Syntax driver with repeat processing.

The OUTPUT(I) subroutine appears as follows.

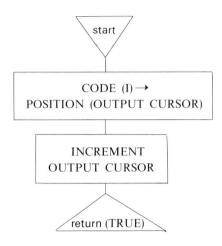

In a previous discussion we considered the coding of a compiler programming language. In particular we used OUTPUT(3) for a programmed
GO TO statement and OUTPUT(4) for an assignment statement. These
code values were specified in syntax equations as follows.

$$\langle\text{go to}\rangle ::= \underline{\text{OUTPUT(3)}}\ \text{GO TO}\ \langle\text{label}\rangle$$

$$\langle\text{assignment}\rangle :: = \underline{\text{OUTPUT(4)}}\ \langle\text{variable}\rangle\ =\ \langle\text{expression}\rangle$$

In tabular form these coding operations will be shown as subroutines
in the syntax tables. For example:

go to	subroutines	OUTPUT(3)
	literal	GO
	literal	TO
	equation	label
	end of table	———
assignment	subroutine	OUTPUT(4)
	equation	variable
	literal	=
	equation	expression
	end of table	———

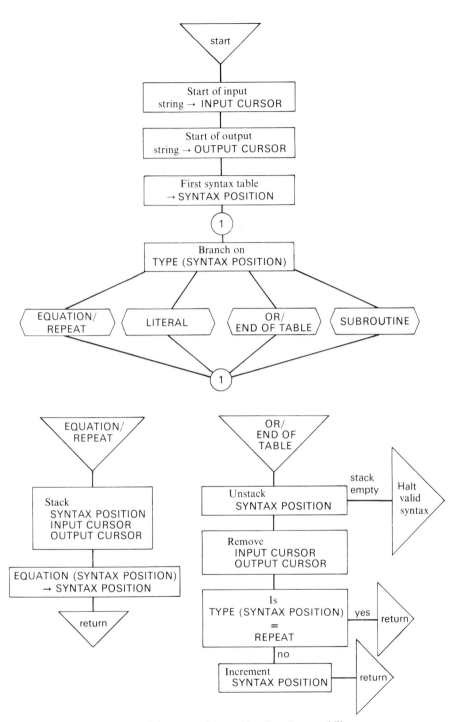

Figure 6.3(a). Syntax driver with subroutine capability.

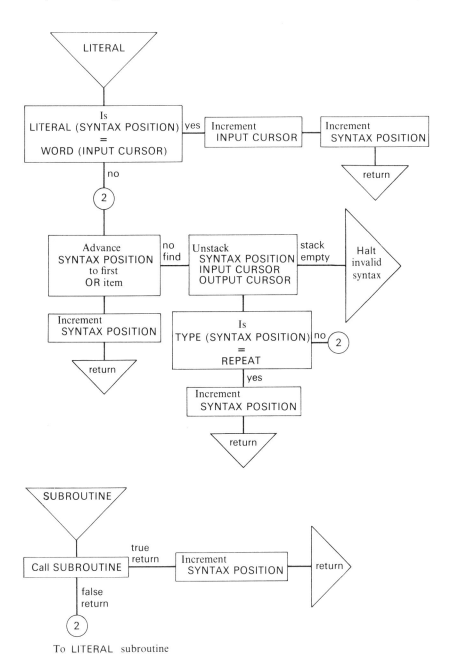

Figure 6.3(b). Syntax driver with subroutine capability.

We will now modify the syntax driver to support such subroutines. As it detects a subroutine entry in the syntax tables the driver now passes control to the specified subroutine. The modified syntax driver, supporting subroutines, appears as shown in Fig. 6.3.

6.6. Summary

Syntax driven methods provide a convenient means for preparing parsing algorithms. A standard syntax driver is used to operate directly on a set of syntax equations. The driver may be used for parsing varied language structures by replacing the driven syntax equations.

The equations are represented in tabular form. The driver matches the form of an incoming programming language to the forms presented in the syntax table, in this way parsing the language. During this parsing process the language may be converted to coded form.

Coded values are generated by syntax subroutines. The coding subroutine is but one example of the generalized subroutine capability. The subroutines have available the means to process input text as well as output text.

A complete preprocessing phase of a language processing system can be constructed from syntax driven methods.

6.7
e x e r c i s e s

(1) How are syntax equations represented in syntax driven algorithms?

(2) What are the primary indicators kept by a syntax driver?

(3) How can "repeat" syntax structures be represented in syntax tables?

(4) How do syntax subroutines interface with the syntax driver?

(5) If you are familiar with assembler macro capabilities, and if your assembler supports macros, try to formulate a syntax equation macro. The purpose of the macro would be to automatically translate an equation into tabular form. You will

probably have to write the equation in some form other than Backus Naur. For example, you might be able to create an IS macro for the following type of syntax equation form.

SENTENCE IS SUBJECT, OR, PREDICATE
SUBJECT IS NOUN PHRASE
:
:

B.

techniques in data management

Let us now turn our discussion to problems in data management. For any application in language processing there is an associated data base. The data might include symbol definitions, information files, or file definitions. In any case, the data must be collected and ordered.

Data items are collected, internal to a programming system, in data tables. We will consider some rather basic properties in ordering and maintaining these tables. We will also consider properties of storage efficiency associated with the table structures.

Of primary interest, however, are the search methods supporting a data structure. It is true that data tables are structured and ordered so that they may subsequently be searched. After all, the purpose of preparing a data structure is to preserve the structure for future use. We will look at several techniques for searching a data structure. Included in these will be some fairly efficient methods for optimizing search timing.

7
data
presentation

Data items are generally presented internally in one of two physical structures: the data table or the data list. In choosing one of the two structures
there are tradeoffs that must be examined. The list provides certain flexibility in arrangement and juxtaposition, whereas the table affords a fast,
clear construction.

7.1. Tables

The data table provides a simple and often used presentation method. A block of computer storage is reserved for the table; tabled items are physically located within that storage block. A pointer at the front of the table serves as a simple and general technique for keeping track of the current extent of the table. The pointer is updated when data items are inserted in or deleted from the table. This form of table is identical to the stack discussed earlier (see Fig. 7.1). In this manner data items are conveniently added to the table, and the *last* item may be conveniently deleted.

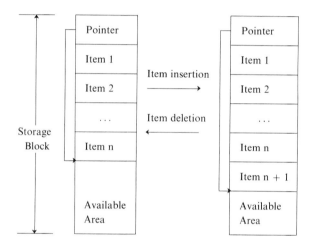

Figure 7.1. Table.

7.2. Lists

The list structure provides greater flexibility in presenting a data module than the table. Rather than physically grouping data items in a common storage block, the list links scattered data items together in the form of a chain. A simple list is chained in one direction in one dimension. Link pointers are physically associated with each data item. The chain begins with the first data item and proceeds by link pointer through the list to the last item. Typically, the link of the last item is set to zero. Data items are inserted in or deleted from the list by breaking and relinking the chain. Figure 7.2 illustrates the list structure.

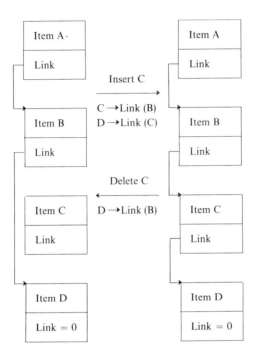

Figure 7.2. List.

7.3. Logical Structure

When choosing a data presentation method the first consideration must be the logical association preserved by the data structure. In this regard, lists provide a more flexible capability than tables. Our previous discussion of lists was limited to one dimensional associations; each list item was associated with one successor item by link pointer. However, the list may be expanded to two or more dimensions by adding link pointers. For example, in the list presentation of a family tree in Fig. 7.3, each data item contains one pointer for maternal association and a second pointer for paternal association.

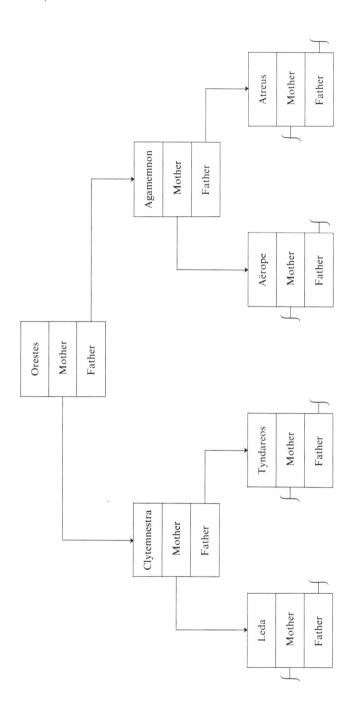

Figure 7.3. Tree structure.

7.4. Maintenance

Language processing systems are particularly susceptible to problems in data base maintenance. The reason for this is that an incoming application language must be continuously reflected in the system tables; the tables must be continuously updated. In an assembler or compiler, new symbol and procedural entries must be processed and applied to existing tables. In picture processing and simulation systems, new display entries or simulation events must be processed and ordered.

7.4.1. Insertion

A form of data base maintenance frequently encountered is data item insertion. As the data base is constructed new data items are inserted into the existing structure. The method of insertion depends on whether the data base is logically ordered. If ordered, the inserted item must be physically placed so as to preserve the proper logical relationships. For example, in a compiler or assembler concordance[1] listing, the symbols are typically printed in alphabetic order. For this purpose the compiler symbol table may be alphabetically ordered. As new symbols are encountered they are inserted into the symbol table in the position dictated by alphabetic collating sequence.

Such an insert into an ordered list is readily processed. The link pointers of the predecessor and successor list items are simply broken and rechained. Schematically this appears as shown in Fig. 7.4.

Inserts to an ordered table are more complicated. The table is ordered by physical ordering of its items. To make space for an insert item, all successor items must be physically pushed down, as Fig. 7.5 shows.

7.4.2. Deletion

A second form of data base maintenance is data deletion. For example, in a conversational compiler the conversational user must be given the ability to alter his programmed algorithm. In particular, he must be able to delete unwanted program statements. To this end the compiler itself sup-

---

[1] The concordance provides a summary listing of all symbols used in a program.

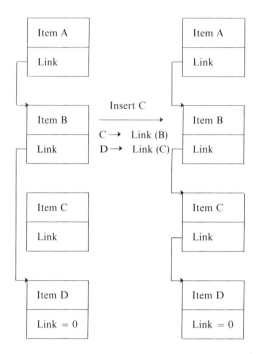

Figure 7.4. Ordered list insert.

ports the deletion of statements from the statement data structure. In general, a list structure is more suitable for data deletion than a table. With a list the deleted data item is simply unlinked from the list chain, as shown in Fig. 7.6.

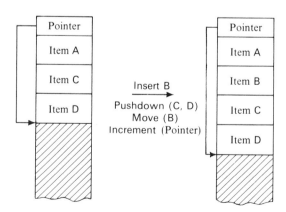

Figure 7.5. Ordered table insert.

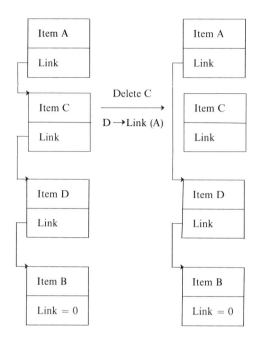

Figure 7.6. List deletion.

When deleting from a table, the vacated table entry remains as a hole in the table storage block. In case of continuous alteration between deletion and insertion, the table storage block will eventually fill and overflow, with

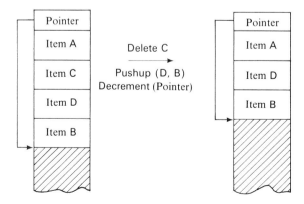

Figure 7.7. Table deletion with pushup.

most storage being taken by unused, vacated areas. One way of resolving this problem is to push up subsequent items when an item is deleted (see Fig. 7.7).

A second and more efficient method for table deletion is possible with fixed length data items. If all items are the same size, the vacated areas resulting from deletions may be saved for future inserts. An auxiliary stack is used for saving the location of vacated areas. Figure 7.8 illustrates this method.

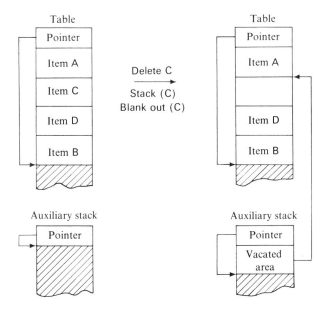

Figure 7.8. Table deletion with auxiliary stack.

With this type of deletion the auxiliary stack keeps a record of vacated areas. When, subsequently, an item is to be inserted in the table, the auxiliary stack is examined first. If available, a vacated area is taken from the stack. Otherwise the table pointer is followed to the next available table area.

7.4.3. Storage efficiency

A maintained data structure is subject to variance in the required storage space. As data items are inserted, the structure expands; as items are deleted, the structure contracts. To optimize storage efficiency across a programmed system, the systems programmer must pay particular attention to these expanding and contracting structures.

The total data storage mechanism should be adjustable. As one structure expands, other data structures should contract to allocate more storage space. Let us consider for a moment the inefficiencies that arise when the structures are not adjustable.

The symbol table and macro table[2] are two major data structures frequently used in an assembler system. If storage area is allocated separately to each, the structures will not be adjustable. When one of the two tables fills, the assembler must stop processing. This will happen even though storage space may still be available in the other table. For example, in Fig. 7.9 the symbol table is full. There is no space for the next programmed symbol encountered. When this symbol occurs the assembly must terminate. It must terminate even when storage space is still available in the macro table.

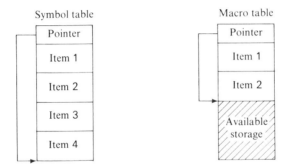

Figure 7.9. Independent tables.

If the tables were adjustable this situation would not arise. The symbol table could begin at the top of storage running down to the macro table; the macro table at the bottom of storage running up. Schematically this appears as shown in Fig. 7.10. Each table would be allowed to expand until the two tables meet. Only then, when all of system storage is taken, would the capacity of either table be exhausted.

---

[2] Assembler systems may provide a macro capability to simplify the generation of frequently used segments of code, thus increasing coding efficiency and readability. To support this capability a system macro table is required.

Symbol table

Figure 7.10. Adjustable tables.

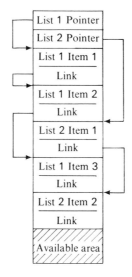

Figure 7.11. Adjustable lists.

For adjusting more than two data structures the structures must be presented in list rather than table form. Several lists may be chained into a common storage area. Figure 7.11 gives an example. Only when this common storage area is exhausted will the storage capacity of any of the lists be exhausted.

7.5. Summary

Two basic methods of presenting a data base are by list or by table structure. Lists provide certain flexibility in logical structure, maintenance, and storage allocation. When this flexibility is not required, the simple and direct table structure may be used.

7.6
exercises

(1) What are two basic methods for internal presentation of a data structure?

(2) What are the advantages and disadvantages of list versus table data structure?

(3) When can an auxiliary stack be used with table deletion?

(4) What are the advantages of using an auxiliary stack with table deletion?

(5) Show how four variable length data structures can be kept in one buffer area.

(6) Show a tree structure for father, son, uncle, and nephew relationships.

8
search structures

Search mechanisms are concerned with the retrieval of a data item from a data structure. In a search environment the data items are identified by keys. For example, a data item in an assembler or compiler symbol table contains the symbol name, together with other information associated with the symbol. The key for the data item is the symbol name. When information about the symbol is desired, the symbol table is searched on that name.

In language processing these search mechanisms are particularly critical. Language processing systems are subject to applications with bulk data processing requirements. Large data structures must be frequently processed and tabulated. In retrieving from these structures the system runs into significant computing requirements.

8.1. Choosing a Search Structure

A search structure consists of a search mechanism together with a data structure method. In general it is not possible to improve the search without improving the data structure.

The systems programmer must be careful in his selection of search structures for a programming system. He must keep in mind overall data processing requirements for the system, not only the search requirements, but also the structure requirements. While he is looking for a method with a fast search mechanism, he must balance this objective with the timings of the associated structure mechanisms, namely, the insert and delete mechanisms.

The choice of a search structure fixes the search, insert, and delete mechanisms for the data base. The speeds of these three mechanisms are the criteria for selecting a search structure. The search, insert, and delete timings are weighted by corresponding system requirements for searching, inserting, and deleting. The search structure that optimizes overall system data processing requirements is the proper search structure for the system.

8.2. Linear Search

Let us use the linear search as an introduction to our discussion of search structures. When we look at any search structure the first topic of discussion will be the supporting data structure.

Given the data structure we can then look at the search, insert, and delete mechanisms. The search mechanism is supported by the data structure; the data structure in turn is built and maintained by the supporting insert and delete mechanisms. In discussing a search structure we will consider the algorithms for these search, insert, and delete mechanisms.

We will also consider the speed of these mechanisms. The actual execution time for a search, insert, or deletion is, of course, dependent on the type of computer the mechanism is programmed for. But rather than consider execution times for a host of varied computers, let us consider a machine-independent representation of execution speeds.

The differences in execution speeds among search structures can be attributed to the number of data items accessed. One type of search mechanism is faster than another because it looks at less data items during the search process. The faster mechanism makes use of its data structure to look only at selected milestone data items when searching the data base. We can then compare the speed of this faster search with that of the slower search by comparing the number of data items accessed. We can also compare insert and delete timings by the same comparison method.

8.2.1. Data structure

Let us now return to the specifics of our linear search structure. In particular, let us consider the supporting data structure.

The linear search mechanism is the only search that requires no special data structure. As a result of this, the linear search is the easiest search to use. It is a natural candidate for any noncritical data module of a programming system.

8.2.2. Search mechanism

A data structure is searched linearly by sequential testing of each data item in the structure. At each test the item key is compared to the target search key. When a match is made, the search is terminated with a find condition. In case there is no matching item in the structure, testing continues to the last data item. When the last item is proven incorrect the search terminates with a no find condition. Tables or lists are linearly searched as shown in Fig. 8.1.

In general the number of items tested in a search environment is dependent on the number of items in the data base. As we consider execution timings for the different search structures we will designate the number of data items in the structure by symbol (N). The timings will then be given as the expected number of items accessed in an N item base.

In this case, with the linear search, the expected number of items tested is $N/2$. On the average, half of the data items have to be tested before the correct item is found.

8.2.3. Insert mechanism

With most search structures, a certain order must be preserved over the data base. When items are added to or deleted from the data base, the data must be reordered. In general this requires the handling of several items within the structure.

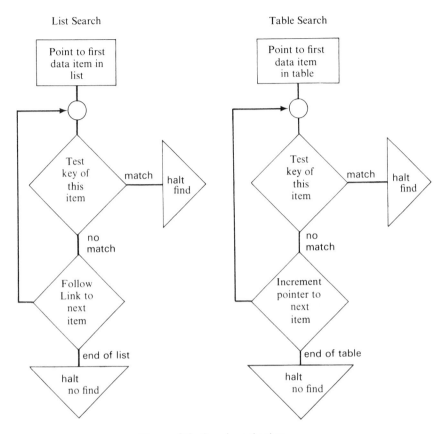

Figure 8.1. Search mechanism.

However, in the particular case of the linear search, there is no ordering of the data base. Data items can be inserted by simple appendage to the end of the data base. Regardless of how many items are in the structure, only one data item is handled: the insert item.

8.2.4. Delete mechanism

In the special case of the linear search the data structure need not be reordered after item deletion. To delete an item, the data structure is first searched on the desired deletion key. The found data item is then removed from the structure. In this process the expected number of data items accessed is $N/2$.

8.3. Binary Search

The binary search provides a fast search mechanism through ordering of the data base. While the search mechanism is fast, the supporting insert and delete mechanisms are slow. As items are added to or deleted from the data base, the data structure must be reordered. This cumbersome reorder process is time consuming.

8.3.1. Data structure

In the binary search structure, data items are ordered on the item keys. The items are held in a table, with items with keys at the low range of the collating sequence at the top of the table and items with larger keys at the bottom.

This ordering is used by the binary search mechanism in searching the table. One requirement for the search is that tabled items be of fixed length; that is, that each table item be the same length as all others. In actual practice, data items may or may not be of fixed length. To satisfy the fixed length requirement with variable length data items, pointers may be used. The table then contains pointers to the data items rather than the data items themselves.

Figure 8.2 gives examples of fixed and variable item tables. In these examples data items are shown with a key and other associated data. As shown, the data structure is ordered on these keys.

8.3.2. Search mechanism

Given the ordering of fixed length data items in a table, we can formulate a search mechanism much faster than was the case for the previous linear search. To motivate this mechanism we consider the following. Given the number (N) of tabled items and the length (L) of each item, the midpoint item of the table can be located. It is at relative table position ($N/2 * L$). The target search key can then be tested against the key of the midpoint data item. If the target key is greater than the midpoint key, then the target item must be in the bottom half of the table; if less, the target item must be in the top half.

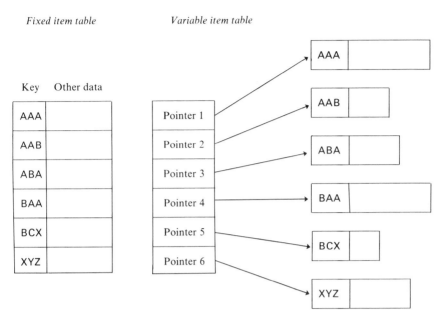

Figure 8.2. Data structure.

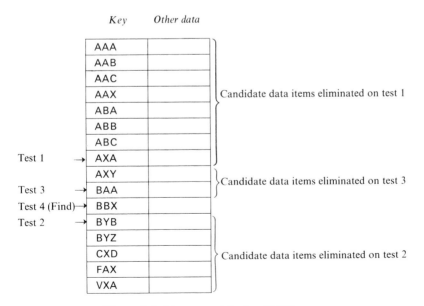

Figure 8.3. Binary search for key (BBX).

With this one calculation and one test the range of candidate data items has been cut in half. There is no need to search any item in that half of the data structure proven out of range. By repeating this process the remaining candidates may again be cut in half; the halving process is repeated until the appropriate data item is isolated. Figure 8.3 is an example of a binary search for the data item with key (BBX). The sixteen item data structure is halved four times in performance of the search.

The search efficiency increases as the data structure grows larger. For example, at most ten tests are required to search a data base of 1024 data items. In general, about $\log_2 N$ tests are required to search a structure of N items.[1]

The search mechanism is shown in flow chart form in Fig. 8.4. The symbols used in this flow chart are

TABLE	Beginning address of ordered table
N	Number of tabled entries
L	Length of each entry
POINTER	Current halving operation table pointer
I	Current iteration number

8.3.3. Insert mechanism

The order of the data table must be preserved during maintenance. When a new data item is inserted in the table, the item must be positioned

---

[1] The exact expected number of tests is somewhat less than $\log_2 N$. The reason for this is that a find could be made on preliminary halving operations. For example, the midpoint item could be the item searched for. If so, only one test would be required for a find. In an N item structure the probability of this is $1/N$. The probability of a find on the second test would be $2/N$, on the third $4/N$, and on the fourth $16/N$. In fact, the probability of a find on the ith test is

$$\frac{2^i}{N} \qquad \text{if } i \le K$$

$$\frac{N - 2^K + 1}{N} \qquad \text{if } i = K + 1$$

$$0 \qquad \text{if } i > K + 1$$

where K is the maximum integer j such that $2^j < N$. The expected number of tests for finding a data item with the binary search is then

$$\frac{1}{N}\left[\sum_{i=1}^{K} i * 2^{(i-1)} + (K + 1) * (N - 2^K + 1)\right]$$

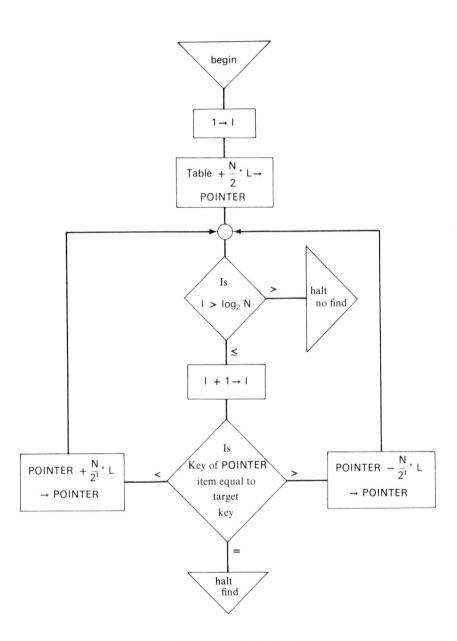

Figure 8.4. Search algorithm.

in its ordered location. Positioning is accomplished by first searching the table to determine where the item belongs. The table is then opened at that position, and the new item inserted. Schematically this procedure appears as shown in Fig. 8.5.

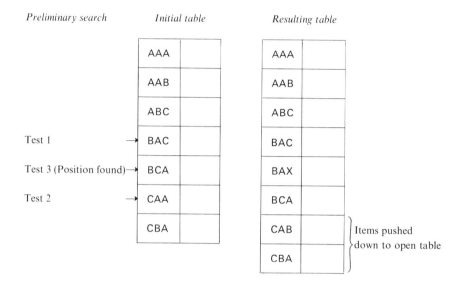

Figure 8.5. Insertion of item (BAX).

Given N items in the data table, the preliminary search will require about $\log_2 N$ tests. To open the table at the insert position, all succeeding data items must be pushed down one place. On the average this pushdown process will move $N/2$ items. The total number of items accessed in the insert is then ($\log_2 N + N/2$). For example, with $N = 1024$, about 522 data items would be accessed during the insert process.

8.3.4. Delete mechanism

When deleting items from the table, a physical table position, previously occupied by the deleted item, is left vacant. If these vacated positions are not filled the efficiency of the structure degenerates. Therefore, it is usually desirable to fill vacated positions by compressing the table after deletion. Schematically the insert process with table compression appears as illustrated in Fig. 8.6.

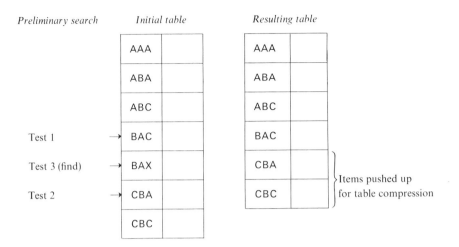

Figure 8.6. Deletion of item (BAX).

The delete mechanism involves a preliminary search to find the deletion item in the table; this search is followed by a table compression. Given N data items in the table, the search will involve about $\log_2 N$ tests, and the compression about $N/2$ moves. The expected number of items accessed in deleting from a binary search table is then ($\log_2 N + N/2$), the same as for an insert.

8.4. Unbalanced Tree Search

The tree search provides, at least logically, the same search mechanism as the binary search. However, it does not use the same data base structure. As a result of this the tree search structure permits the same search speed as the binary search, but much faster insert and delete mechanisms.

8.4.1. Data structure

By use of a special list structure the halving operations of the binary search mechanism are preset into the data base. Each data item contains a left link pointer to data items of lower keys, and a right link pointer to data items with higher keys. An example is given in Figure 8.7.

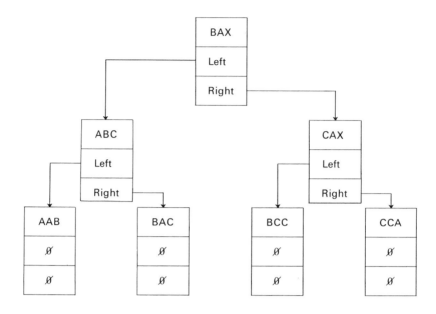

Figure 8.7. Tree structure.

The entire list structure is called a *tree*; each data item in the tree is called a *node*. The tree has one special node called the *root*. In Fig. 8.7 node(BAX) is the root. It serves as the base or beginning of the tree.

The ordering of the tree becomes evident by looking at its relation to the root. All nodes left of root(BAX) contain lower keys: AAB, ABC, and BAC. All nodes to the right contain higher keys: BCC, CAX, and CCA. This same ordering relation holds for nodes of the tree other than the root. For example, lower key AAB is left of node ABC, and higher key BAC is right. The relation of this ordering to our previous binary search table ordering is shown in Fig. 8.8.

8.4.2. Search mechanism

The search of a tree begins at the root node. The target search key is compared to the root node key; if it is greater the node right of the root is examined; if less the node left of the root is examined. This process continues until the desired node is found. Figure 8.9 gives the flow chart form for the search algorithm.

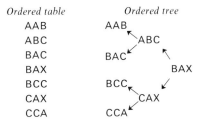

Figure 8.8. Comparison of ordered table to ordered tree.

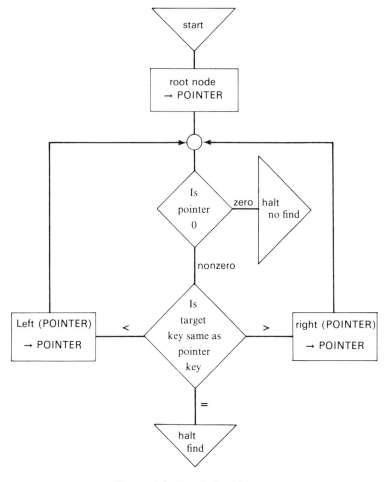

Figure 8.9. Search algorithm.

The efficiency of this search algorithm is dependent on how well the tree is balanced. For the present we will say a tree is well balanced if, for each node in the tree, the number of nodes linked left is approximately equal to the number linked right. Examples of a well balanced and poorly balanced tree are shown in Figs. 8.10 and 8.11.

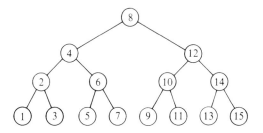

Figure 8.10. Well balanced tree.

The poorly balanced trees require more tests in searching. In our two examples, Fig. 8.10 requires at most four tests to find any node; whereas Fig. 8.11, in the case of nodes 10 and 12, may require as many as nine tests. The expected number of tests in searching a well balanced tree with N nodes

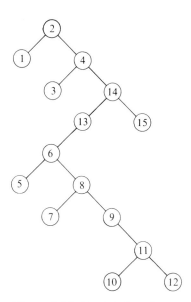

Figure 8.11. Poorly balanced tree.

is about $\log_2 N$. However, as the tree becomes imbalanced, this figure becomes larger. For example, in Fig. 8.11 the expected number of search tests is 5.07, as compared to 3.26 for its balanced mate in Fig. 8.10.

8.4.4. Insert mechanism

The structure of a tree is such that an insert node will always belong at the bottom of the tree. Therefore an insert simply consists of searching the tree to see where the insert node belongs and then linking the node into the structure. The order of the tree is in this way naturally preserved. However, what may not be preserved is the balance of the tree. Our insert mechanism only places nodes in the tree in the proper collating order. In doing this it does not ensure a well balanced structure.

For an example let us look at an assembler system. A tree structure could be used for the assembler symbol table. As symbols are encountered in the assembled program they would be inserted in the tree. Consider an application in which the following sequence of symbols is encountered: L4, L2, M2, L1, M1, L3, M3. Our insert mechanism would then build a tree through a corresponding sequence of insert operations (see Fig. 8.12).

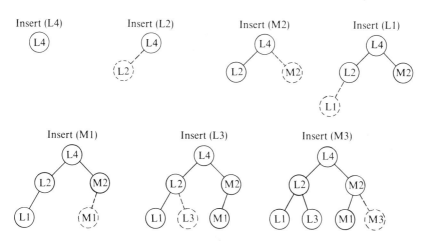

Figure 8.12. Building a tree.

Now let us consider the symbols in a more likely sequence, namely: M1, M2, M3, L1, L2, L3, L4. The corresponding sequence of inserts yields a tree that is not so well balanced (see Fig. 8.13).

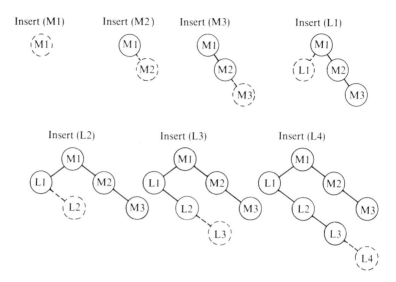

Figure 8.13. Building a typical symbol tree.

Remember that imbalance of the tree structure has a degrading effect on search efficiency. For this reason the unbalanced tree search structure is not optimally efficient for language processing symbol tables. Programmers have a custom of using symbol sequences like L1, L2, L3, etc. This custom limits the efficiency of the search mechanism.

8.4.4. Delete mechanism

In contrast to insert nodes, which are always added to the bottom of the tree, deletion nodes may be taken anywhere from the tree. In particular there is no reason why the root node cannot be deleted.

In the case of deleting an interior tree node, in particular the root node, the basic structure of the tree is threatened. Without a root the tree would be split in two. Fortunately this problem is readily sidestepped by swapping a bottom level node for the deleted interior node. For example, in the deletion in Fig. 8.14, node(7) is swapped for node(8).

The deletion mechanism first requires a preliminary search to find the deletion node in the tree. If this node is in the interior of the tree it is then swapped with an appropriate bottom level node. If the deletion node is initially at the bottom it is simply unlinked. As with the insert mechanism,

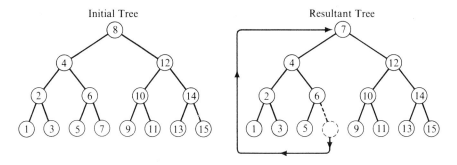

Figure 8.14. Deletion of node(8).

this delete mechanism does not ensure a well balanced tree. However, if the tree is well balanced, only $\log_2 N$ item accesses are required to delete a node.

8.5. Balanced Tree Search

For general application of the tree search structure, the tree can be re-balanced after each insert and deletion. A continuous balanced tree ensures optimum search results.

Unfortunately, the balance mechanisms are complicated. They require an in-depth methodology for structuring and restructuring the tree. At this time we give you, the reader, fair warning of the complexity of the following sections. We suggest you reserve their reading for a time when you can chart balanced structures. If this is not the time you can go on to Section 8.6.

8.5.1. Data structure

The tree structure will be basically the same as that previously discussed, the difference being that the structure will be kept in balance. For this purpose a *balance indicator* will be kept for each node of the tree. This indicator will specify the current state of balance or imbalance of the associated node.

The balance indicator for a node depends on the chain of nodes linked to the left and to the right of that node. To define the balance indicator we must first define the properties of a node chain. We will define tail(X) as a chain of nodes leading from node(X) to the bottom of the tree.

To clarify this definition let us look at tails in a specific tree (Fig. 8.15).

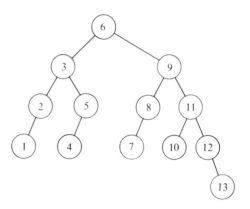

Figure 8.15. Tree.

In this tree node(9) has three tails: chain(9, 8, 7), chain(9, 11, 10), and chain(9, 11, 12, 13). Node(3) has two tails: chain(3, 2, 1) and chain(3, 5, 4).

Let us define left(X) as the node linked to the left of node(X) and right(X) as the node linked right. For example, in the tree in Fig. 8.15 left(6) = 3, right(6) = 9, and left(10) = ∅.

Now we can define the balance indicator for a nodeX. The indicator will contain one of three values (left, right, or balance) according to the following conditions.

Left: A nodeX will be called left heavy if the longest tail(left(X)) is longer than the longest tail(right(X)).

Right: A nodeX will be called right heavy if the longest tail(right(X)) is longer than the longest tail(left(X)).

Balance: A nodeX will be said to be balanced if the longest tail(left(X)) is the same length as the longest tail(right(X)).

For example, in Fig. 8-15 the balance indicator for node(6) is right. This is true because of the following. Of the two tails(left(6))—chain(3,2,1) and chain(3,5,4)—the longest contains three nodes. Of the three tails(right(6))—chain(9,8,7), chain(9,11,10), and chain(9,11,12,13)—the longest contains four nodes. Therefore the longest tail(right(6)) is longer than the longest tail(left(6)). Node(6) is balanced right. In fact, our sample tree with all balance indicators inserted appears as shown in Fig. 8.16. For ease in presentation we will abbreviate left, right, and balance as L, R, and B, respectively.

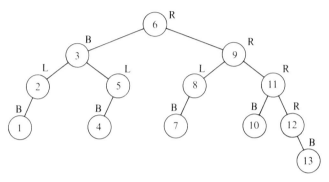

Figure 8.16. Tree with balance indicators.

To ensure a fair balance of the total tree structure we will impose the following restriction.

For any nodeX, the longest tail(left(X)) will differ in length by no more than one node from the longest tail(right(X)).

This still permits left heavy and right heavy nodes; however, they cannot be heavy by more than length one. Figures 8.17 and 8.18 are examples of legal and illegal tree structures, respectively.

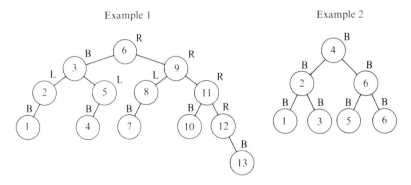

Figure 8.17. Legal structures.

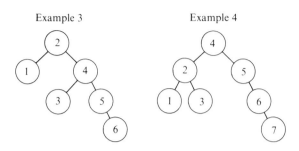

Figure 8.18. Illegal structures.

Examples 1 and 2 in Fig. 8.17 are legal structures because no nodes in either structure are left or right heavy by more than length one. In Fig. 8.18, Example 3 is illegal because node(2) is right heavy by length two; Example 4 because node(5) is right heavy by length two.

8.5.2. Search mechanism

The restriction on the tree structure balance ensures an efficient search mechanism. The search algorithm is the same as that used for the unbalanced tree structure. The balanced structure yields an expected number of nodes tested of about $\log_2 N$ when searching an N node tree.

8.5.3. Insert mechanism

The insert mechanism is also the same as that for the unbalanced tree. The structure is first searched to determine where the insert item belongs; the insert item is then linked into the tree. It is assigned an initial balance indicator of B. What differs is that the tree, if necessary, is to be rebalanced after the insert.

Recall the list structure supporting a tree. Items are collected in inter-related chains through left and right link pointers. The basis of the forth-coming balance algorithm is that large sections of the tree can be adjusted into balance by resetting only a few link pointers. The problem is to find which links to reset. For example, consider the insertion of node(9) in the tree in Fig. 8.19. The balance indicators in the tree are those that existed before the insert.

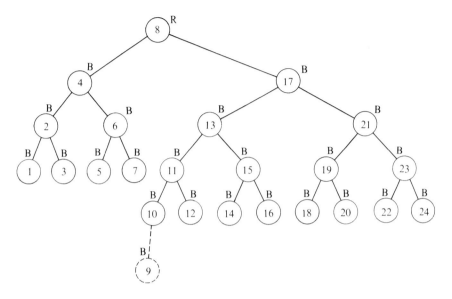

Figure 8.19. Insertion of node(9).

Before insertion the tree is legitimately balanced. However, after insertion, root node(8) is right heavy by length two. Now we have to determine how to rebalance. At first glance it looks like a difficult problem. There are now too many nodes to the right of the root. No matter what adjustment is done, the root will still be right heavy by length two.

The only solution to this is to change the root by making 9 or 10 or some higher node the root. In fact, we will make node(13) the new root. The required change in link pointers to accomplish this is certainly not obvious. However, the changes are quite simple computationally. Only four links have to be reset. They are as follows.

$$8 \rightarrow \text{Left}(13)$$
$$17 \rightarrow \text{Right}(13)$$
$$15 \rightarrow \text{Left}(17)$$
$$11 \rightarrow \text{Right}(8)$$

The resulting tree is then as shown in Fig. 8.20.

As stated, the problem in balancing a tree is to find which links are to be reset. We will have to introduce just a few new concepts in order to prepare a procedure for finding those links.

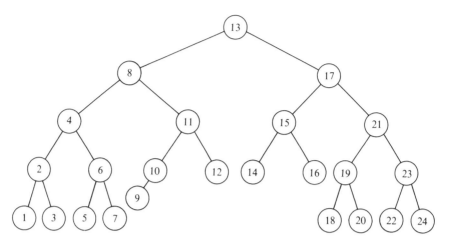

Figure 8.20. Balanced tree.

We define the path as the chain of nodes linking the root node to the inserted node. In the above example, before rebalancing, the path was chain(8, 17, 13, 11, 10, 9). This path, together with the balance indicators in the tree, is used to find a focal point for rebalancing the tree. The focal point is the first node encountered, working up from the bottom of the path, with a balance indicator other than B. Note that in our example this node was the root node(8). This root was, in fact, the focal point used when we rebalanced the tree.

Given the focal node we must then determine which links are reset in balancing the tree. We must also specify which balance indicators must be reset in the balanced tree. The easiest way of discussing this is mathematically rather than by text description.

8.5.4. Mathematical notation

The above discussion serves as groundwork for the mathematical balancing algorithm. Just a few additional definitions are necessary for its formulation.

Path: Defined, as previously, as the chain of nodes linking the root node to the insert node.

Path nodes: Nodes on the path will be designated by symbols $(X_1, X_2, \ldots, X_n)$—the root as X_1, and the insert node as X_n. In our example Fig. 8.19 these designations would be

X_1 node(8)
X_2 node(17)
X_3 node(13)
X_4 node(11)
X_5 node(10)
X_6 node(9)

Focal node: As before the focal node will be defined as the first path node out of balance. Mathematically the focal node is defined as follows. Let f be the smallest i such that indicator(X_j) equals B for $j = i + 1, \ldots, n$. The focal node is then X_f.

P-Direction: For any nodeX_i in the path, define the path direction at X_i as *left* if X_{i+1} is left of X_i. P-Direction is *right* if X_{i+1} is right of X_i. These direction values will be abbreviated as L and R. In our sample structure the path directions are as follows.

P-direction (8)   R
P-direction (17)   L
P-direction (13)   L
P-direction (11)   L
P-direction (10)   L

P-link: For any nodeX_i in the path, P-link(X_i) is defined as the link pointer in X_i that points to X_{i+1}. In our example P-link(8) = 17 and P-link(11) = 10.

Q-link: For any nodeX_i in the path, define Q-link(X_i) as the link pointer in X_i that does not point to X_{i+1}. In our example Q-link(8) = 4 and Q-link(11) = 12.

8.5.5. Assignment notation

To balance a tree, certain alteration assignments must be made. These include the resetting of link pointers and balance indicators. To present the balance algorithm, we need a notation for the assignments. The following type of notation will be used.

$B \rightarrow$ indicator(X_i):   The balance indicator of node(X_i) is set to B.

$X_i \rightarrow$ P-link(X_j): The link pointer in node(X_j), which used to point to X_{j+1}, is set to point at X_i.

P-direction$(X_i) \rightarrow$ indicator(X_j): The balance indicator of node(X_i) is set equal to the path direction at X_j.

P-link$(X_i) \rightarrow$ Q-link(X_j): The link pointer in node(X_j), which did not point to X_{j+1}, is set to point at X_{i+1}.

8.5.6. Balance algorithm

Before applying the balance algorithm, the insert node has already been linked to the bottom of the tree and assigned an initial balance indicator of B. We are now only concerned with balancing the tree.

The balance algorithm must first chart and save the path nodes $X_1, X_2, \ldots, X_n$. While doing this it can also determine the focal node X_f. Then, based on conditions about X_f, there are five cases for the algorithm to consider.

Case 1: If $f = 0$, then
 P-direction$(X_i) \rightarrow$ indicator(X_i) for $1, 2, \ldots, n - 1$

Case 2: If P-direction$(X_f) \neq$ indicator(X_f), then
 B $\rightarrow$ indicator(X_f)
 P-direction$(X_i) \rightarrow$ indicator(X_i) for $i = f + 1, \ldots, n - 1$

Case 3: If P-direction$(X_f) =$ indicator(X_f) and P-direction(X_f)
 $=$ P-direction(X_{f+1}) then
 B $\rightarrow$ indicator(X_f)
 Q-link$(X_{f+1}) \rightarrow$ P-link(X_f)
 $X_f \rightarrow$ Q-link(X_{f+1})
 $X_{f+1} \rightarrow$ P-link(X_{f-1})
 P-direction$(X_i) \rightarrow$ indicator(X_i) for $i = f + 2, \ldots, n - 1$

Case 4: If P-direction$(X_f) =$ indicator(X_f) and P-direction(X_f)
 $\neq$ P-direction(X_{f+1}) and P-direction$(X_f) =$ P-direction(X_{f+2}) then
 P-direction$(X_{f+1}) \rightarrow$ indicator(X_f)
 Q-link$(X_{f+2}) \rightarrow$ P-link(X_f)
 $X_{f+3} \rightarrow$ P-link(X_{f+1})
 $X_f \rightarrow$ Q-link(X_{f+2})
 $X_{f+1} \rightarrow$ P-link(X_{f+2})
 $X_{+2} \rightarrow$ P-link(X_{f-1})
 P-direction$(X_i) \rightarrow$ indicator(X_i) for $i = f + 3, \ldots, n - 1$

Case 5:   If P-direction(X_f) = indicator(X_f) and P-direction(X_f)
      $\neq$ P-direction(X_{f+1}) and P-direction(X_f) $\neq$ P-direction(X_{f+2}) then
      B $\rightarrow$ indicator(X_f)
      P-direction(X_f) $\rightarrow$ indicator(X_{f+1})
      X_{f+3} $\rightarrow$ P-link(X_f)
      Q-link(X_{f+2}) $\rightarrow$ P-link(X_{f+1})
      X_f $\rightarrow$ P-link(X_{f+2})
      X_{f+1} $\rightarrow$ Q-link(X_{f+2})
      X_{f+2} $\rightarrow$ P-link(X_{f-1})
      P-direction(X_i) $\rightarrow$ indicator(X_i) for $i = f + 3, \ldots, n - 1$

Case 1 example

In Case 1 the insert did not adversely affect the balance of the tree structure. As a result no link pointers need resetting; only the balance indicators require alteration. For an application of the Case 1 balance algorithm, consider the insert of node(4) in Fig. 8.21.

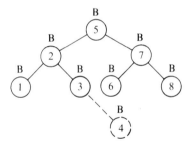

Figure 8.21. Insert node(4).

The path is charted as $X_1 = 5$, $X_2 = 2$, $X_3 = 3$, and $X_4 = X_n = 4$. Since there is no path node with indicator other than B, the focal nodeX_f is nonexistent (f = 0). In this case the balance algorithm calls for setting the balance indicators of the first n − 1 path nodes to their path direction. This is done as follows.

           L $\rightarrow$ indicator(5)
           R $\rightarrow$ indicator(2)
           R $\rightarrow$ indicator(3)

Figure 8.22 represents the resulting tree.

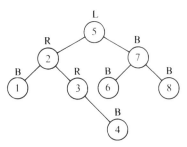

Figure 8.22. Resulting tree.

Case 2 example

In Case 2 there is also no requirement for adjusting the tree structure. Let us assume a Case 2 balance is to be applied after the insert of node(11) (Fig. 8.23). The path is charted as $X_1 = 7$, $X_2 = 9$, $X_3 = 10$, and $X_4 = X_n = 11$. The focal node is then the first unbalanced path node: $X_f = 7$. Note that, since direction $(X_f) = R$ is different from indicator$(X_f) = L$, this is in fact a Case 2 balance problem.

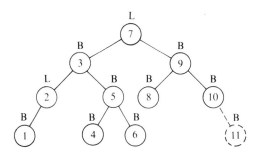

Figure 8.23. Insert node (11).

The Case 2 balance algorithm calls for the following balance indicator settings.

$$B \rightarrow \text{indicator}(X_f)$$
$$\text{direction}(X_i) \rightarrow \text{indicator}(X_i) \text{ for } i = f + 1, \ldots, n - 1$$

These assignments are made for our sample problem as follows:

$$B \rightarrow \text{indicator}(7)$$
$$R \rightarrow \text{indicator}(9)$$
$$R \rightarrow \text{indicator}(10)$$

Figure 8.24 shows the resulting tree.

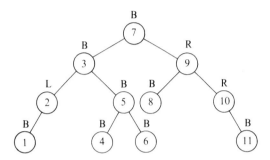

Figure 8.24. Resulting tree.

Case 3 example

In Case 3 we can see a structure adjustment performed by the balance algorithm. For an example let us apply the algorithm to the insert of node(13) in Fig. 8.25.

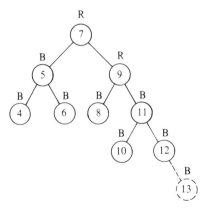

Figure 8.25. Insert node (13).

The path is charted as $X_1 = 7$, $X_2 = 9$, $X_3 = 11$, $X_4 = 12$, and $X_5 = X_n$ $= 13$; the focal node as $X_f = 9$. Notice that the focal node is initially balanced heavy to the right (to the side of the insert). When the new node is inserted the focal node will become unbalanced by length 2. As a result the tree must be adjusted back into proper balance. The assignments to do this, together with the Case 3 algorithm commands, appear as follows.

Algorithm command	*Sample structure assignment*
B → indicator (X_f)	B → indicator(9)
Q-link (X_{f+1}) → P-link (X_f)	10 → right(9)
X_f → Q-link (X_{f+1})	9 → left(11)
X_{f+1} → P-link (X_{f-1})	11 → right(7)
direction (X_i) → indicator (X_i)	R → indicator(12)
for $i = f + 2, \ldots, n - 1$	

These assignments produce the tree in Fig. 8.26.

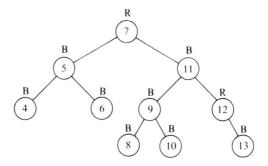

Figure 8.26. Resulting tree.

Case 4 example

In Case 4 the tree must also be adjusted back into balance. For an example, consider the insert of node(11) in Fig. 8.27. In this example, the path is $X_1 = 7$, $X_2 = 9$, $X_3 = 12$, $X_4 = 10$, $X_5 = X_n = 11$. The focal node is $X_f = 9$. The Case 4 balance algorithm calls for the following balance operations.

Algorithm command	*Sample structure assignment*
P-direction (X_{f+1}) → indicator (X_f)	L → indicator (9)
Q-link (X_{f+2}) → P-link (X_f)	𝘽 → right (9)
X_{f+3} → P-link (X_{f+1})	11 → left (12)
X_f → Q-link (X_{f+2})	9 → left (10)

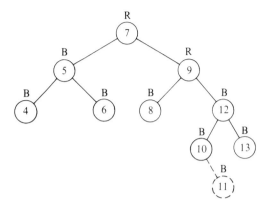

Figure 8.27. Insert node (11).

$$X_{f+1} \rightarrow \text{P-link} (X_{f+2})$$
$$X_{f+2} \rightarrow \text{P-link} (X_{f-1})$$
P-direction $(X_i) \rightarrow$ indicator (X_i)
    for $i = f + 3, \ldots, n - 1$

$12 \rightarrow \text{right} (10)$
$10 \rightarrow \text{right} (7)$
No operation

Figure 8.28 shows the resulting tree.

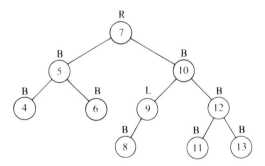

Figure 8.28. Resulting tree.

Case 5 example

The final case of the balance algorithm is Case 5. For its application consider the insert of node(10) in Fig. 8.29. In this example the path is

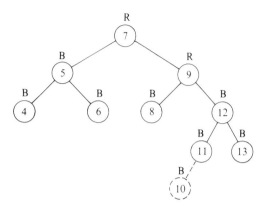

Figure 8.29. Insert node (10).

$X_1 = 7$, $X_2 = 9$, $X_3 = 12$, $X_4 = 11$, and $X_5 = X_n = 10$; the focal node is $X_f = 9$. The tree is balanced as follows.

Algorithm command	Sample structure assignment
B → indicator (X_f)	B → indicator (9)
P-direction (X_f) → indicator (X_{f+1})	R → indicator (12)
X_{f+3} → P-link (X_f)	10 → right (9)
Q-link (X_{f+2}) → P-link (X_{f+1})	Ø → left (12)
X_f → P-link (X_{f+2})	9 → left (11)
X_{f+1} → Q-link (X_{f+2})	12 → right (11)
X_{f+2} → P-link (X_{f-1})	11 → right (7)
direction (X_i) → indicator (X_i)	No operation
for $i = f + 3, \ldots, n - 1$	

After these operations the tree appears as shown in Fig. 8.30.

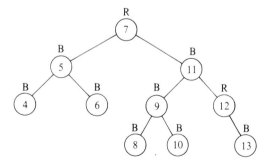

Figure 8.30. Resulting tree.

8.5.7. Insert timing

Item insert to the balanced tree structure requires a preliminary search followed by a balance operation. The search requires the testing of about $\log_2 N$ items of an N item structure. In the worst case the balance operation references $2 * \log_2 N + 5$ items. Together, the search and balance reference at most $3 * \log_2 N + 5$ data items. In actual practice the expected number of items accessed is less than this. On the average about $\log_2 N + 6$ items are handled.

8.5.8. Delete mechanism

The delete mechanism operates from the bottom of the tree structure. If the deletion node is initially located in the interior of the tree it is swapped with a bottom level node. For example, in the tree shown in Fig. 8.31, node(4) is deleted by replacement with node(5). In this replacement node(5) assumes the left and right links and the balance indicator of node(4). The position occupied by the replacement node will be called the *deletion position*.

Initial Tree

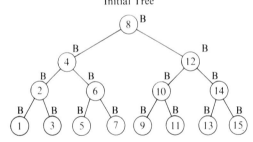

Resulting Tree

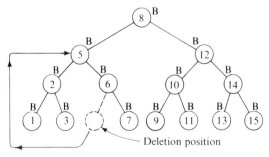

Deletion position

Figure 8.31. Deletion of node (4).

After deletion, the tree is rebalanced about the deletion position. Notice that in the resultant tree (Fig. 8.31) the balance indicator of node(6) is improper. All that is required to resolve this tree is to change that balance indicator. In general, however, the structure may have to be adjusted back into proper balance.

This balance, after item deletion, is more complicated than the previous balance after insert. In that mechanism a tree was brought back into balance by locating a proper focal position, then making an adjustment about that position.

To restore balance after item deletion, a series of adjustments may be required. These include an *initial* adjustment at the deletion position followed by a series of *prime* and *auxiliary* adjustments.

As before, a path is charted that links the deletion position to the tree root. In our sample tree in Fig. 8.31 the path is $X_1 = 8, X_2 = 5, X_3 = X_n = 6$. Prime adjustments are made about a series of focal nodes leading up this path. Auxiliary adjustments are made about a series of focal nodes leading back down from a prime.

These adjustment positions are shown schematically in Fig. 8.32. This chart shows the set of all possible adjustment positions. In actual practice adjustments may not, and most probably will not, be required at all positions. A proper balance algorithm must provide a mechanism for selecting those positions that require adjustment. It must then be able to make the selected adjustments. The forthcoming balance algorithm will be prepared

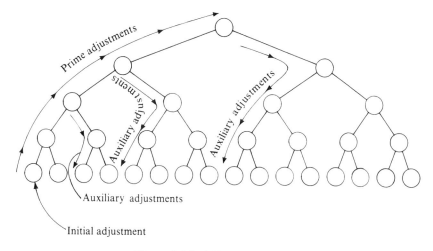

Figure 8.32. Adjustment positions.

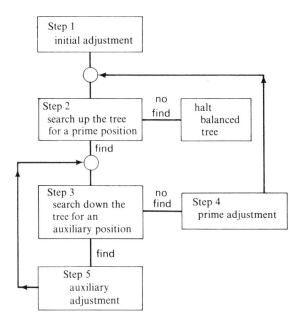

Figure 8.33. Balance algorithm.

along these lines. Its five steps will be as follows.

Step 1: Initial adjustment
Step 2: Search up the tree for a prime position
Step 3: Prime adjustment
Step 4: Search down the tree for an auxiliary position
Step 5: Auxiliary adjustment

These five steps, brought together, form a complete balance algorithm. Step 1 is applied first to make the initial adjustment. Step 2 is applied to find a proper prime position. Then, before each prime adjustment is made, Steps 4 and 5 are applied. In block chart form this appears as illustrated in Fig. 8.33.

8.5.9. Delete timing

Item deletion requires a preliminary search to find the deletion position. This search accesses about $\log_2 N$ data items. Following the search and deletion, the balance algorithm is applied.

In the worst case the balance algorithm requires an adjustment at each adjustment position in the tree. Given N items in the tree, there are about $(\log_2 N)^2/2$ such positions. For example, if $N = 1024$ there are about fifty positions. However the expected number of adjustments is only about three. Since adjustment involves the alteration of about eight structure pointers, the expected number of structure items accessed during the balance is $3*8 = 24$. On the average about $\log_2 N + 24$ items are accessed during the combined delete and balance.

8.5.10. Mathematical notation for the balance after delete algorithm

The notation used for our balance after delete algorithm is much the same as for the previous balance after insert algorithm. The only basic difference is the use of Q-direction. The same path($X_1, X_2, \ldots, X_n$) of nodes is used, and the same P-direction over this path. The new term, Q-direction, is defined as follows. It carries one of two values according to the path direction.

Left: The Q-direction of a node X_i will be left if node(X_{i+1}) is right of X_i.

Right: The Q-direction of a node X_i will be right if node(X_{i+1}) is left of X_i.

8.5.11. Mathematical algorithm

The path($X_1, X_2, \ldots, X_n$) is the chain of nodes linking the root node to the insert position. This path is used in the five steps of the balance algorithm. As we look at each step of the algorithm, we will consider examples of its application.

Step 1: initial adjustment

In Step 1 the initial adjustment about the insert position is made. There are three cases for this adjustment. In one case, when indicator(X_n) = B, the initial adjustment terminates the balance process. The following is the Step 1 algorithm.

Case 1: If indicator(X_n) = B, then
$\quad\quad$ Q-direction(X_n) → indicator(X_n)
$\quad\quad$ Halt (balanced tree)
$\quad\quad$ End

Case 2: If indicator(X_n) = P-direction(X_n) then
$\quad\quad$ B → indicator(X_n)
$\quad\quad$ n − 1 → f
$\quad\quad$ Go to Step 2
$\quad\quad$ End

Case 3: If indicator(X_n) = Q-direction(X_n), then
$\quad\quad$ B → indicator(Q-link(X_n))
$\quad\quad$ If P-direction(X_n) = L then
$\quad\quad$ X_n → left(right(X_n))
$\quad\quad$ End
$\quad\quad$ If P-direction(X_n) = R then
$\quad\quad$ X_n → right(left(X_n))
$\quad\quad$ End
$\quad\quad$ Q-link(X_n) → P-link(X_{n-1})
$\quad\quad$ $\emptyset$ → Q-link(X_n)
$\quad\quad$ B → indicator(X_n)
$\quad\quad$ n − 1 → f
$\quad\quad$ Go to Step 2
$\quad\quad$ End

Let us look at a sample application of Step 1. Consider the deletion of node(1) from the tree in Fig. 8.34. In this example the path is charted as

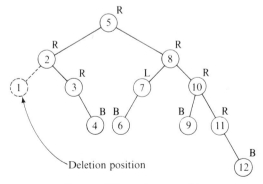

Figure 8.34. Delete node (1).

$X_1 = 5$ and $X_2 = X_n = 2$. Since indicator$(X_n) = R$ is the same as Q-direction$(X_n) = R$, this is an example of the third case. The alterations for Step 1, together with the resulting tree, are as follows.

Algorithm command	*Sample structure assignment*
B → indicator (Q-link (X_n))	B → indicator (3)
X_n → left (right(X_n))	2 → left (3)
Q-link (X_n) → P-link (X_{n-1})	3 → left (5)
$\emptyset$ → Q-link (X_n)	$\emptyset$ → right (2)
B → indicator (X_n)	B → indicator (2)
$n - 1$ → f	1 → f
Go to step 2	

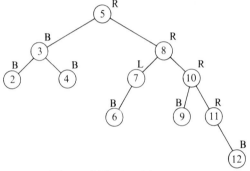

Figure 8.35. Resulting tree.

Notice that in the resulting tree node(5) is right heavy by length 2. To resolve this condition the Case 3 algorithm sets the focal position to X_{n-1}, in this case node(5), and passes control to Step 2.

Step 2: search for prime position

In Step 2 the focal position is pushed up the path in search of a prime position. If, in the process of this search, a balanced node or the end of tree is encountered, the balance process is terminated. The Step 2 algorithm appears as follows.

Case 0: If f = 0, then halt (balanced tree)
Case 1: If indicator(X_f) = B then
         Q-direction(X_f) → indicator(X_f)
         Halt (balanced tree)
         End

Case 2:   If indicator(X_f) = P-direction(X_f) then
                     B → indicator(X_f)
                     f − 1 → f
                     Go to Step 2
                     End

Case 3:   If indicator(X_f) = Q-direction(X_f) then
                     Go to Step 3
                     End

Our previous sample tree is an example of Step 2, Case 3. Step 2 is called with focal node(5). When the algorithm discovers that indicator (X_f) = R is the same as Q-direction(X_f) = R, control is passed to Step 3.

Step 3: prime adjustment

Step 3 makes a prime adjustment on the focal node. In one special case, Case 1 of Step 3, a call must first be made to Step 4. In this case auxiliary adjustments must be made before the prime adjustment can be carried out. Following is the Step 3 algorithm. In this algorithm symbols Y and Z are used as working variables.

Case 1:   If indicator(Q-link(X_f)) = P-direction(X_f) then
                     Call Step 4 (Q-link(X_f), new root)
                     new root → Q-link(X_f)
                     Go to Case 2
                     End

Case 2:   If indicator(Q-link(X_f)) ≠ P-direction(X_f) then
                     Q-link(X_f) → Y
                     Y → P-link(X_{f-1})
                     If P-direction(X_f) = R then
                     right(Y) → Z
                     X_f → right(Y)
                     End
                     If P-direction(X_f) = L then
                     left(Y) → Z
                     X_f → left(Y)
                     End
                     Z → Q-link(X_f)
                     If indicator(Y) ≠ B then

$$B \rightarrow indicator(X_f)$$
$$B \rightarrow indicator(Y)$$
$$f - 1 \rightarrow f$$
Go to Step 2
End
If indicator(Y) = B then
  $$Q\text{-direction}(X_f) \rightarrow indicator(X_f)$$
  $$P\text{-direction}(X_f) \rightarrow indicator(Y)$$
Halt (balanced tree)
End

Our sample problem falls under Case 2 of Step 3. Recall that the tree was passed to Step 3 in the state shown in Fig. 8.36. A prime adjustment is

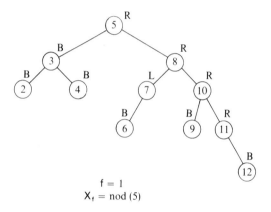

f = 1
X_f = nod (5)

Figure 8.36. Tree passed to Step 3.

to be made to node(X_f). Since indicator (Q-link(X_f)) = R is different than P-direction(X_f) = L, a Case 2 prime adjustment is called for. This adjustment is carried out as follows.

Algorithm command	*Sample structure assignment*
Q-link (X_f) → Y	8 → Y
Y → P-link (X_{f-1})	8 → root
Since P-direction (X_f) = L, then	
left (Y) → Z	7 → Z
X_f → left (Y)	5 → left (8)
Z → Q-link (X_f)	7 → right (5)
Since indicator (Y) ≠ B then	
B → indicator (X_f)	B → indicator (5)
B-indicator (Y)	B → indicator (8)
$f - 1 \rightarrow f$	0 → f
Go to Step 2	

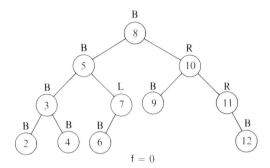

Figure 8.37. Adjusted tree.

You will notice that this structure is now properly balanced. This condition is recognized by our balance algorithm when control is passed to Step 2, with $f = 0$.

Step 4 : auxiliary adjustments

It is sometimes necessary to make auxiliary adjustments. Step 4 is available for this purpose. This step accepts as input a subtree of root root. It adjusts the subtree, giving it a new root such that indicator(new root) $\neq$ indicator(root). An example of this adjustment operation is given in Fig. 8.38.

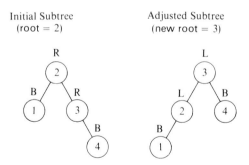

Figure 8.38. Step 4 operation.

For this adjustment we will define four new terms.

T-direction : T-direction = indicator (root).
U-direction : U-direction = L if indicator (root) = R ;
       U-direction = R if indicator (root) = L.

T-link : For any node X define T-link(X) as left(X) if indicator (root) = L; as right(X) if indicator (root) = R.

Q-link : For any node X define Q-link(X) as left(X) if indicator (root) = R; as right(X) if indicator (root) = L.

The adjustment algorithm itself will be recursive. As secondary adjustments are required for the initial adjustment, the algorithm will call itself. The following is this algorithm.

Recursive procedure Step 4 (root, new root)
Case 1:   If indicator (T-link(root)) = U-direction then
    Call Step 4 (T-link (root)), new root)
    new root → T-link (root)
    Go to Case 2
    End
Case 2:   If indicator (T-link (root)) ≠ U-direction then
    T-link (root) → new root
    If indicator (new root) = B then B → indicator (root)
    If indicator (new root) ≠ B then U-direction → indicator (root)
    U-direction → indicator (new root)
    U-link (new root) → T-link (root)
    root → U-link (new root)
    Return (new root)
    End

Figure 8.39 is an example of the application of the Step 4 algorithm. In this example the initial subtrees, the adjustment operations, and the adjusted subtree are shown.

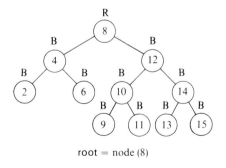

root = node (8)

Figure 8.39. Initial subtree.

Algorithm command	*Sample structure assignment*
Since indicator (T-link(root)) ≠ U-direction	
T-link (root) → new root	12 → new root
B → indicator (root)	B → indicator (8)
U-direction → indicator (new root)	L → indicator (12)
U-link (new root) → T-link (root)	10 → right (8)
root → U-link (new root)	8 → left (12)
Return (new root)	

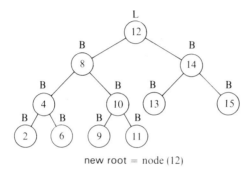

new root = node (12)

Figure 8.40. Adjusted subtree.

Step 4 concludes our discussion of the balance mechanism. The tree structure, balanced after each insert and deletion, provides a fast, generalized search method. For many system applications the balanced binary tree provides the best solution to system data processing problems.

8.6. Hash Total Search

Hash total techniques take a different approach to the search environment. Here the target search key is converted, or hashed, into a direct table address. This address is then used to locate the proper data item.

There are a great many variations to the hash total method. In fact, a method is generally tailored for each search application. In this book we will only consider one method. This is done to give you a basic feeling for hash techniques. It is not our purpose to set forth precise programming methods.

In a hash total environment the data items are held in an M position hash table. At search time the target key is hashed to the address of the appropriate table position. One way of performing this hash is to divide the key by M and take the division remainder as the candidate hash position.

If there are N data items under consideration, it is customary to allot more than N positions to the hash table, say, $1.3 * N$. Even so, this does not prevent hashing of two different keys to the same table position. This is called a collision.

When upon inserting an item in the hash table a collision occurs, the problem encountered is what to do with the insert item. Collisions may be resolved in several ways, the simplest of which is to keep a separate table for collision items. Items of duplicate hash position are then placed in this collision table.

For an example of a hash structure let us consider a special computing machine. In this machine the numeric value of character A will be 1, B = 2, C = 3, and D = 4. The value of a character string will be the decimal value of the corresponding string of numbers. For example:

$$ABC = 123$$
$$DAAC = 4113$$
$$BCA = 231$$

For this machine consider an eight position hash table. The hash position for some data item (X) will then be remainder$(X/8)$. For example:

$$hash(ABC) = remainder(123/8) = 3$$
$$hash(AAA) = remainder(111/8) = 7$$
$$hash(CBA) = remainder(321/8) = 1$$
$$hash(BAC) = remainder(213/8) = 5$$
$$hash(CBC) = remainder(323/8) = 3$$

If items were inserted in the hash table in the above order, the last item would cause a collision with the first. It would be placed in the collision table. The resulting hash structure would then be

Hash table		Collision table
Position	Item	Item
0		CBC
1	CBA	
2		
3	ABC	
4		
5	BAC	
6		
7	AAA	

The specific hash algorithm chosen generally represents the best tradeoff in storage requirement and search time. As the hash table is expanded the probability of a collision is reduced. This in turn reduces the size of the collision table, thus reducing search time.

Actually, there are several ways to tradeoff search, insert, and deletion timing with available storage space. For this reason there is no general set of timings applicable for all hash algorithms.

In summary, we will show the search, insert and delete mechanisms for the hash total structure in flowchart form (Figs. 8.41, 8.42, and 8.43).

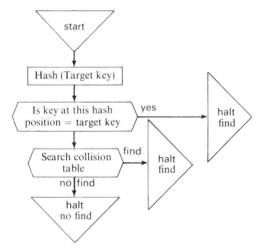

Figure 8.41. Search mechanism.

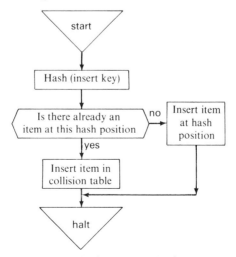

Figure 8.42. Insert mechanism.

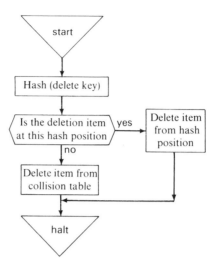

Figure 8.43. Delete mechanism.

Since there are many variations to these mechanisms, they are charted only generally.

8.7. Summary

This section presents a summary of the important aspects of each search technique. The section is concluded with technique timing charts.

Linear search:
   best insert timing
   worst search timing
   near worst delete timing
   (trivial to implement)

Binary search:
   worst insert timing
   good search timing
   worst delete timing

Unbalanced tree search:
   good insert timing

good search timing
good delete timing
(These timings are optimal timings approached only under favorable circumstances.)

Balanced tree search:
good insert timing
good search timing
good delete timing
(difficult to implement)

Hash total search:
Timing characteristics may be tailored by tradeoffs in storage space and hash methods. If there is an abundance of storage space a superior hash algorithm can always be constructed.

Figures 8.44, 8.45, and 8.46 are respective graphical comparisons of the search, insert, and deletion timings for each search structure. Timings are presented in terms of the number of data items accessed. Accesses are plotted as a function of the number of data items in the structure. Both scales of each graph are logarithmic.

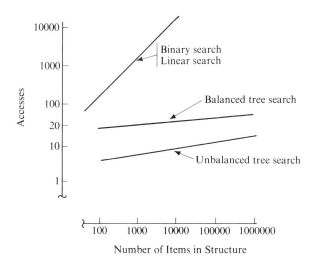

Figure 8.44. Deletion timing.

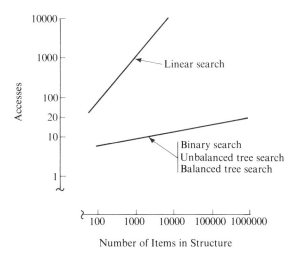

Figure 8.45. Search timing.

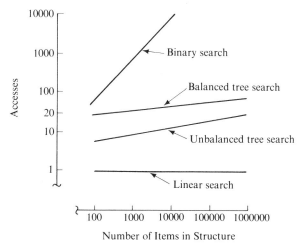

Figure 8.46. Insert timing.

8.8
e x e r c i s e s

(1) How can the efficiency of a search structure be measured?

(2) Given an N item data base, what are the expected number of items accessed in a

search, insert, and deletion for the linear search, binary search, and balanced tree search structures?

(a) N = 100
(b) N = 1000
(c) N = 10000

(3) Consider the unbalanced tree insert mechanism. Show the tree built from a sequence of inserts corresponding to the following data item keys.

(a) 10,15,12,17,6,2,16,18,14,1,3,11
(b) 1,2,3,4,5,6,10,11

(4) Consider the balanced tree insert mechanism. Show, at each step, the tree built from a sequence of inserts corresponding to the following data item keys: 1,2,3,4,5,6, 10,11.

(5) Show the balancing steps of the balanced tree delete mechanism for deletion of node (1) from the tree in Fig. P8.1.

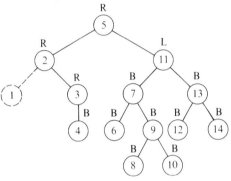

Figure P8.1.

(6) Consider hash methods for an information file keyed on part serial numbers. The file contains 1000 parts.

(a) Show a hash structure when each serial number is exactly eight characters long.
(b) Show a hash structure for variable length part numbers.

(7) Consider an assembler symbol table. Assume assembled programs are to be 1000 statements long. Every fifth statement will declare a new symbol; every statement will reference a symbol.

(a) In processing a program each newly declared symbol is inserted in the symbol table; each referenced symbol requires a symbol table search. What are the approximate data processing requirements for each of the following symbol table structures?

(i) Linear search structure
(ii) Binary search structure
(iii) Balanced tree search structure

(b) Assume you have chosen a balanced tree structure for the symbol table. At the completion of the assembly the symbols will be listed in alphabetical order in a concordance table. Show an algorithm for extracting symbols from the tree in alphabetical order.

(c) What drawback can you see in using a hash structure for the symbol table?

(8) For the assembler symbol table of Question 7, we have limited storage space. In calculating the total storage space required for each search structure, assume the following. Symbols will contain no more than eight characters. In a list structure, each link pointer will require the equivalent of two characters of storage space.

(a) If each symbol is eight characters long, what is the total storage requirement for 1000 symbols for each of the following search structures?
   (i) Linear search
   (ii) Binary search
   (iii) Balanced tree search

(b) If symbols are of variable length and the average length is four characters, what is the total storage requirement for 1000 symbols for the same structures?
   (i) Linear search
   (ii) Binary search
   (iii) Balanced tree search

(c) Consider the use of a hash structure for 1000 symbols. If you allot 1300 positions to the hash table and 200 positions to the collision table, what is the total storage requirement
   (i) If all symbols are eight characters long?
   (ii) If symbols are variable length, with an average length of four characters?

C.

application

Our initial and continuing objective in preparing this book is pragmatic presentation. We wish to describe methods in language processing that will get the job done. To accomplish this, a thorough knowledge of programming techniques must be balanced by an overriding understanding of how and where those techniques are used. Even the most complete compendium of technical information is of little practical value without the total framework in which this information is ordered. The purpose of this final section of the book is to present a gross framework for language processing; the presentation is an analysis of a sample program application. We feel this section is necessary to order and merge the techniques discussed in the earlier sections.

The techniques will be applied to a sample problem in processing basic compiler statements; the solution of the problem should result in a compiler system. Development of the system will be split into three phases: definition, design, and implementation. During the definition phase the compiler will be described from an external viewpoint—the system will be formulated from the standpoint of how it is to be used. Next, a system design will be constructed to formulate and describe the system from an internal viewpoint —the design will act as a plan for implementing the system. Finally, selected techniques will be applied to the design plan to bring about system implementation. These three steps circumscribe the practical necessities in developing a programming system. Every attempt will be made to keep the discussion at a useful rather than theoretical level.

9
definition of a
sample compiler system

The first step taken in solving a programming problem is to determine what the problem is. To this end a complete functional definition is prepared. The system is functionally declared from the viewpoint of the user, thus defining the requirements of the total system and therefore the goals and objectives of the programming effort. The functional definition of our sample compiler system will demonstrate, by example, how the definition may be formulated.

We will consider a subset of a scientific compiler. The compiler could be in FORTRAN, ALGOL, or PL1; most of the subset under consideration is present in each. Our compiler subset will support six basic programming statements: READ, PRINT, ASSIGN, GO TO, DO, and IF. These six statements cover the basic provisions for entering data to a programmed algorithm, performing arithmetic and logical computations and manipulation of the data, and displaying results.

The description of these statements circumscribes the functional definition of our system. Statements are built up from functions and expressions; functions and expressions, in turn, are built up from constants and program variables. The constants and variables are the basic elements of the system. They will serve as a starting point for our discussion.

9.1. Program Variables

During the processing of a programmed algorithm, the results of intermediate computations are held in, or assigned to, program variables. For example, the statement $X = 2 * Y + 3$ multiplies the value of variable (Y) by 2, adds 3, and assigns the result to variable (X). In our compiler, variables may be assigned arithmetic or Boolean values. To permit a quick, clear discussion of the system we will not consider character string, floating point, or array capabilities.

As in FORTRAN, the variables used in a programmed algorithm need not be declared. Internally Boolean and numeric variables look the same. A Boolean TRUE is designated by the arithmetic value 1, FALSE by 0. Conversely, nonzero arithmetic values may be considered as having the Boolean value TRUE, arithmetic zero the Boolean value FALSE. The composition of a variable is determined by its use in the program statement. The variable itself has no composition property; it may be used as Boolean or numeric. Some legal values for a program variable are

29	(TRUE)
−413	(TRUE)
0	(FALSE)
7	(TRUE)
1	(TRUE)

9.2. Program Expressions

Arithmetic or Boolean expressions may be formed over the program variables in the usual manner. Boolean and arithmetic operators available for this purpose are

Arithmetic operators	Boolean operators
+ prefix and infix plus	& and
— prefix and infix minus	| or
* multiply	= equal
/ divide	≠ not equal
≠ exponentiate	> greater
	< less
	≥ greater or equal
	≤ less or equal

9.2.1. Operator priorities

Operators of an expression are normally evaluated in a left-to-right order. This order is modified by the following evaluation priorities.

Priority 1
— prefix minus, as in −4
+ prefix plus, as in +7

Priority 2
↑

Priority 3
*
/

Priority 4
— infix minus, as in X − 2
+ infix plus, as in Y + 5

Priority 5
=
≠
>
<
≥
≤

Priority 6
&
\|

9.2.2. Parenthetical usage

Parentheses may be used within an expression to override all orders of operator evaluation. Examples of ordinary parenthetical expressions are

Arithmetic expressions	*Boolean expressions*
X + 3*Y	X > 14
14	Y + 17 < 2 + X ↑ 4
− 2*(X + Y ↑ 3)	X = 6|Y ≤ 2
	(A|B) & Y = 6
	A

9.2.3. Composition properties

In actual practice the composition (arithmetic or Boolean) of an expression is determined by its use within the program statement. For our compiler we will permit the programmer to mix arithmetic and Boolean values. This provides the additional flexibility (which the programmer may or may not choose to use) of writing the following type of expressions.

Expression	*Value*
(X > Y)*4	4 if X > Y, otherwise 0
(A|B)*7	7 if A or B is true, otherwise 0
IF X − 14	Equivalent to IF X ≠ 14
IF (X > Y)*6 − Z	Equivalent to IF (X > Y&Z ≠ 6)|(X ≤ Y&Z ≠ 0)

9.3. Functions

Four built-in functions are supported by our compiler to show the use of function calls in an expression. A function may be used as an operand in an expression; for example, 3*SQRT(X) + 7 or 2*MIN(X,Y,Z). Functions assume the functional value of their arguments. For example, SQRT(16) assumes the value (4) or MIN(3, − 7) assumes the value (− 7). The assumed value is then used as the operand within the expression. Thus 3*SQRT(16) + 2 = 3*4 + 2 = 14.

Expressions are used as arguments to a function. Each argument is separated by commas. For example, MIN(X ↑ 2 + 3,Y − 4) or MAX(X,Y,O) or SQRT(Y/3 − 1). The four functions supported are

MAX(X,Y,Z...)
  Assumes the maximum value of its argument list

MIN(X,Y,Z...)
  Assumes the minimum value of its argument list

ABS(X)
  Assumes the absolute value of the single argument

SQRT(X)
  Assumes the square root of the single argument

9.4. Statements

Now we must look at the statements for our compiler. Program statements are built up from functions and expressions.

9.4.1. Assignment statement

The basic processing statement of any compiler is the assignment statement. It assigns the value of an expression to a program variable.

Examples
X = 7
A = 1
Y = 4*(X − 2)
B = X > Y&Z≠7
RATE = 3 + SQRT(TIME − 7)

Syntax
⟨assignment⟩ ::= ⟨variable⟩ = ⟨expression⟩

9.4.2. GO TO statement

The natural order of statement execution in a program is sequential. The first program statement is executed first, then the second, then the third, etc. However, the programmer may anticipate conditions that require alteration in the execution sequence; in such cases control must be transferred to some area of the program other than the next sequential statement. The GO TO statement is available for this purpose. Labels or tags may be assigned to a statement, as in

$$LABEL: X = Y \uparrow 2 + 3$$
$$L1: \qquad Y = 7$$

Control may then be transferred to such statements by GO TO, as in

$$GO \ TO \ LABEL$$
$$GO \ TO \ L1$$

The syntax of the GO TO statement is

$$\langle go \ to \rangle :: = GO \ TO \ \langle label \rangle$$

9.4.3. DO statement

The DO statement provides another method for controlling statement execution sequence. Associated with each DO statement is an END statement. All program statements between DO and END are said to be in the scope of the DO.

$$DO \ I = 1 \ TO \ 5 \ BY \ 1$$
$$Scope \begin{cases} SQUARES \ SQUARES + I \uparrow 2 \\ CUBES \ CUBES + I \uparrow 3 \end{cases}$$
$$END$$

The DO statement provides iteration control over its scope. All statements in the scope are repeatedly executed until iteration control terminates. Iteration control is governed by the I = 1 TO 5 BY 1 clause. Variable (I) is initially assigned value (1). At each iteration, variable (I) is incremented BY 1 until it reaches 5; at that time statement execution sequence drops through the END statement, following completion of the last scope iteration. An equivalent algorithm to the above would be

$$I = 1$$
$$LOOP: \quad IF \ I > 5 \ THEN \ GO \ TO \ END^1$$

---

[1] The IF clause is explained in detail in Section 9.4.5.

```
            SQUARES = SQUARES + I ↑ 2
            CUBES = CUBES + I ↑ 3
            I = I + 1
            GO TO LOOP
        END:    . . .
```

In either case the algorithm forms the sum of I ↑ 2 in SQUARES and the sum of I ↑ 3 in CUBES.

```
        SQUARES = 1 ↑ 2 + 2 ↑ 2 + 3 ↑ 2 + 4 ↑ 2 + 5 ↑ 2
        CUBES = 1 ↑ 3 + 2 ↑ 3 + 3 ↑ 3 + 4 ↑ 3 + 5 ↑ 3
```

Up to this point we have considered single DO statements. It is quite permissible to nest DO statements within other DO statements. For example:

```
        DO I = 1 TO 5 BY 1
            PRODUCT = I
            DO J = I + 1 TO I + 2 BY 1
                PRODUCT = PRODUCT*J
            END
            PERMUTATIONS = PERMUTATIONS + PRODUCT
        END
```

This algorithm computes the number of statistical permutations in drawing four objects from a group of eight objects. PERMUTATIONS = (1*2*3 + 2*3*4 + 3*4*5 + 4*5*6 + 5*6*7). In fact, the permutation algorithm for drawing M from N objects is

```
        DO I = 1 TO N − M + 1 BY 1
            PRODUCT = I
            DO J = I + 1 TO I + M − 2 BY 1
                PRODUCT = PRODUCT*J
            END
            PERMUTATIONS = PERMUTATIONS + PRODUCT
        END
```

In the above examples we have used the standard form of the DO statement: DO I = (initial value) TO (final value) BY (increment value). This standard form provides the complete control information for a DO statement. However, there are frequently used standard forms that could be made available in convenient default forms. For example, the value (1) is frequently used as the increment value. In our compiler value (1) will be the default increment value of the BY N clause; if BY N is not specified, BY 1 is assumed. For example:

Default form	*Standard form equivalence*
DO I = 1 TO 4	DO I = 1 TO 4 BY 1
DO J = X ↑ 2 + 2 TO Y	DO J = X ↑ 2 + 2 TO Y BY 1

A second convenient form of default is available for specifying an iteration count only. Frequently a programmer wishes to loop through a set of statements a certain number (N) of times. This may be done by DO N.

Default form	*Standard form equivalence*
DO 7	DO DUMMYVARIABLE = 1 TO 7 BY 1
DO N/5 + 3	DO DUMMYVARIABLE = 1 TO N/5 + 3 BY 1

A final default form is available for conditional execution sequence control. Frequently a program is written to execute a series of statements only if some condition is true. In this case the series of statements may be grouped by a DO — END pair. The DO is then conditionally executed with an iteration count of 1. For example:

```
IF ⟨condition⟩ THEN DO 1
    ⟨statement series⟩
END
```

When using the DO statement with an iteration count of 1 the count may be omitted; the default value is 1.

Default form	*Standard form equivalence*
DO	DO DUMMYVARIABLE = 1 BY 1 TO 1

As a brief summary, the following are examples of the four forms of the DO statement.

```
DO I = 1 TO 6 BY 1
    . . .
    . . .
END
```

This assigns an initial value of 1 to variable (I). Statements in the DO range are repeatedly executed; the value of I is incremented BY 1 at each iteration. When I reaches 6, the final iteration is processed, and control drops through the END statement.

$$DO \ I = 1 \ TO \ 6$$
$$\ldots$$
$$\ldots$$
$$END$$

This is identical to the previous example.

$$DO \ 6$$
$$\ldots$$
$$\ldots$$
$$END$$

This is also identical to the first example, except the value of variable (I) is not altered or available to other statements of the program.

$$IF \ X > 4 \ THEN \ DO$$
$$\ldots$$
$$\ldots$$
$$END$$

This executes statements of the DO scope only if X > 4. The following is the syntax for the DO statement.

$$\langle do \rangle ::= DO \ \langle variable \rangle = \langle expression \rangle \ TO \ \langle expression \rangle$$
$$BY \ \langle expression \rangle \ |$$
$$DO \ \langle variable \rangle = \langle expression \rangle \ TO \ \langle expression \rangle \ |$$
$$DO \ \langle expression \rangle \ |$$
$$DO$$

9.4.4. Input/Output statements

To enter data to a programmed algorithm, or to display results, input and output statements are available. Examples are

READ(X)
> Accepts an entry from the input device, converts to internal arithmetic form, and assigns the value to variable (X)

PRINT(A)

Converts the value of variable(A) to external form and prints the result on the output device

READ(A,B,X,Y,Z)

Accepts five entries from the input device, converts to internal form, and assigns corresponding values to variables A,B,X,Y, and Z

PRINT(X∗14,Z∗2 −1)

Computes the value of expressions X∗14 and Z∗2 −1 and displays those values at the output device

The syntax for input/output statements is

$$\langle read \rangle :: = READ\ (\ \langle variable \rangle \int [\ ,\langle variable \rangle])$$
$$\langle print \rangle :: = PRINT\ (\ \langle expression \rangle \int [\ ,\langle expression \rangle])$$

9.4.5. IF clause

Any of the previous statements may be executed conditionally. The IF clause specifies a Boolean expression that must be true for the statement to be executed. Statements without IF clauses are called simple statements; with IF clauses, they are called compound. Examples of compound statements are

IF X > Y THEN Z = 2

If the value of variable (X) is greater than the value of variable (Y), then 2 is assigned as the value of variable (Z) ; otherwise no action is taken.

IF X = Y THEN GO TO L1

Statement execution control is passed to the statement labeled L1 if variable (X) has the same value as variable (Y).

IF A THEN DO

If A has the Boolean value (TRUE), then statements within the scope of the DO will be executed; otherwise execution control will drop through the matching END statement.

The syntax for the IF clause is

$$\langle if \rangle :: = IF\ \langle expression \rangle\ THEN\ \langle simple\ statement \rangle$$

9.5. Program Example

Our compiler, as defined, provides the basic capabilities for creating a programmed algorithm to process arithmetic computations and display results. An example of such an algorithm follows. The algorithm computes the square root of a number (N) through three successively closer approximations.

(1)   READ(N)
(2)   ROOT = N
(3)   IF N < 2 THEN GO TO L2
(4)   ROOT = N /2
(5)   I = 1
(6)   L1: ROOT = (ROOT + N /ROOT) /2
(7)   I = I + 1
(8)   IF I ≤ 3 THEN GO TO L1
(9)   L2: PRINT(ROOT)

A statement-by-statement trace of the algorithm shows the way the computation is performed as the algorithm is executed. For this trace we will assume a value of 100 for N.

Statement number	Action taken as statement is executed
(1)	N = 100
(2)	ROOT = 100
(3)	No action
(4)	ROOT = 50
(5)	I = 1
(6)	ROOT = (50 + 100/50) /2 = 26
(7)	I = 2
(8)	Control is transferred to L1
(6)	ROOT = (26 + 100/26) /2 = 14
(7)	I = 3
(8)	Control is transferred to L1
(6)	ROOT = (14 + 100/14) /2 = 10
(7)	I = 4
(8)	No action
(9)	10 is displayed

This algorithm could be simplified by using a DO statement. This is done by substituting a DO statement for statements 5, 7, and 8. The resulting algorithm is logically equivalent.

```
(1)    READ(N)
(2)    ROOT = N
(3)    IF  N < 2 THEN  GO  TO  L2
(4)    ROOT = N /2
(5)    DO  I = 1  TO  3
(6)    ROOT = (ROOT + N /ROOT) /2
(7)    END
(8)    L2:   PRINT(ROOT)
```

For those programmers who do not like the use of tags and GO TO statements, a second DO may be used. It replaces statement 3.

```
READ(N)
ROOT = N
IF  N < 2 THEN  DO
    ROOT = N /2
    DO  3
        ROOT = (ROOT + N/ROOT) /2
    END
END
PRINT(ROOT)
```

Finally, the two DO statements may be compacted into one by use of mixed mode Boolean and arithmetic expressions.

```
READ(N)
ROOT = N /2*(1 + (N < 2))
IF  N ≥ 2 THEN  DO
    ROOT = (ROOT + N /ROOT) /2
END
PRINT(ROOT)
```

This algorithm enters the value of N from the input device. In the second statement ROOT is initialized to N if N < 2; otherwise, ROOT is assigned the value N/2. The DO structure is executed only if N ≥ 2. Thus, if N = 0 or 1, no computation is necessary, and control drops through to the PRINT statement. For values of N larger than 1, computation is necessary and is effected by iteration of the statement ROOT = (ROOT + N/ROOT)/2.

9.6. System Syntax

At this stage of problem definition the overall context and objective of the system is clear. The system accepts programmed statements to perform computations directed by those statements. The overall form for these statements has been presented, but the exact structure for preparing a statement has not yet been described. To this end a formal syntax of the programming language is declared. The syntax equations given below precisely pinpoint which forms may, and which may not, be used in preparing a programmed algorithm.

$\langle$statement$\rangle$ :: = $\langle$label$\rangle$: $\langle$command$\rangle$; | $\langle$command$\rangle$;
$\langle$command$\rangle$ :: = $\langle$simple$\rangle$ | $\langle$compound$\rangle$
$\langle$compound$\rangle$ :: = IF $\langle$expression$\rangle$ THEN $\langle$simple$\rangle$
$\langle$simple$\rangle$ :: = $\langle$read$\rangle$ | $\langle$print$\rangle$ | $\langle$assign$\rangle$ | $\langle$do$\rangle$ | $\langle$go to$\rangle$ | $\langle$end$\rangle$
$\langle$read$\rangle$ :: = READ ($\langle$variable$\rangle$ ∫ [, $\langle$variable$\rangle$])
$\langle$print$\rangle$ :: = PRINT ($\langle$expression$\rangle$ ∫ [, $\langle$expression$\rangle$])
$\langle$assign$\rangle$ :: = $\langle$variable$\rangle$ = $\langle$expression$\rangle$
$\langle$goto$\rangle$ :: = GO TO $\langle$label$\rangle$
$\langle$do$\rangle$ :: = $\langle$count$\rangle$ | $\langle$index$\rangle$
$\langle$count$\rangle$ :: = DO $\langle$expression$\rangle$ | DO
$\langle$index$\rangle$ :: = DO $\langle$variable$\rangle$ = $\langle$expression$\rangle$ TO $\langle$expression$\rangle$ BY $\langle$expression$\rangle$ |
              DO $\langle$variable$\rangle$ = $\langle$expression$\rangle$ TO $\langle$expression$\rangle$
$\langle$end$\rangle$ :: = END

$\langle$expression$\rangle$ :: = $\langle$operand$\rangle$ ∫ [$\langle$infix operator$\rangle \langle$operand$\rangle$]
$\langle$operand$\rangle$ :: = $\langle$prefix operator$\rangle \langle$prime$\rangle$ | $\langle$prime$\rangle$
$\langle$prime$\rangle$ :: = $\langle$constant$\rangle$ | $\langle$variable$\rangle$ | $\langle$function$\rangle$ | $\langle$subexpression$\rangle$
$\langle$subexpression$\rangle$ :: = ($\langle$expression$\rangle$)
$\langle$function$\rangle$ :: = $\langle$function name$\rangle$ ($\langle$expression$\rangle$ ∫ [, $\langle$expression$\rangle$])
$\langle$function name$\rangle$ :: = MIN | MAX | ABS | SQRT
$\langle$label$\rangle$ :: = $\langle$symbol$\rangle$
$\langle$variable$\rangle$ :: = $\langle$symbol$\rangle$
$\langle$symbol$\rangle$ :: = $\langle$alpha$\rangle$ ∫ $\langle$alphanumeric$\rangle$
$\langle$constant$\rangle$ :: = ∫ $\langle$numeric$\rangle$
$\langle$alphanumeric$\rangle$ :: = $\langle$alpha$\rangle$ | $\langle$numeric$\rangle$
$\langle$alpha$\rangle$ :: = A | B | C | . . . | Y | Z
$\langle$numeric$\rangle$ :: = 1 | 2 | 3 | . . . | 9 | 0
$\langle$infix operator$\rangle$ :: = + | − | * | / | ↑ | = | ≠ | < | > | ≤ | ≥
$\langle$prefix operator$\rangle$ :: = + | −

The system syntax augments text description of the language processing system. Text description introduces and outlines the system; the syntax clarifies and completes the system definition. Together they prescribe the precise forms and functional capabilities available to users of the system.

9.7. Programmer Interaction

It is now clear what statements and what forms of those statements are acceptable to the compiler system. What is not clear is the way statements are presented to the system, whether in batch mode or interactively through on-line consoles.

Batch mode processing has been the method employed by many language processing systems. Here the programmer submits his application problem, in its entirety, to the system. He receives, in return, the problem results. The programmer has no control over the actual processing of his algorithm.

The lack of programmer control in batch processing may be contrasted to the availability of programmer control in interactive processing. As interactive facilities become more and more prevalent, the human being is put into the process for interfacing with and directing his application problem. From his remote console[2] the programmer interacts with the language processing system, directing the structure and execution of his problem. Our sample compiler will be designed for interactive operation.

9.8. Summary

The first stage of effort in the development of a language processing system is a functional definition. The definition provides the requirements of the total system, and therefore the goals and objectives of the development effort. Of concern in a functional definition is the format and operation of the supported programming language. This format is presented first in

---

[2] In this context we define remote console as a decentralized device (for example, teletype or cathode ray tube) capable of direct communication with the computer.

text description and then summarized in a set of syntax equations. The net result of the functional definition is a complete description of the use and processing requirements of the programming language. It provides a definition point and a goal for system design and development.

10
elements
of design

Before looking at the design of our sample compiler, let us consider the general concepts important in the design of a programming system. The purpose of design is to formulate a plan for construction and implementation of the system. This plan must be made in a clear, concise presentation. It serves as a definition point for system development.

10.1. Task Segmentation

An effective plan must declare methods and procedures for each segment of the system. Note that the important consideration here is the system segment. Development plans cannot be formulated and isolated in specific segments without a definition point telling what those segments are. The first and primary order of business in system design is a division of the system effort into well-defined segments. Each segment serves as a separate development task; the formulation and resolution of all tasks comprise the resolution of the system.

As an example of task segmentation let us consider a project that is easily understood: the construction of a house. We could divide the construction effort into nine segments.

Prepare foundation
Erect frame
Shingle roof
Enclose with siding
Install plumbing
Install electrical system
Install heating system
Panel interior
Paint

Each segment could then be approached and resolved separately. The overall construction plan would be a composite of the plans for all segments.

10.1.1. Logically complete segments

When a system effort is divided into smaller tasks, the boundary of division is not arbitrarily taken. It is chosen to provide a clean, logical break between system segments. Each segment should stand as a complete logical entity, not as a fragmentary collection of disassociated work units.

The segments serve as a definition point for the system. Each must comprise a conceptual entity that is readily understood. In this way several persons can visualize the breakdown of effort in producing the system. For example, our house construction effort is broken down by segment and could be allocated to professionals of varied skills and talents. Masonry workers could contract for the foundation task, carpenters for the frame, electricians for the electrical work, etc. To facilitate such a distribution, the work units of each task are declared a logical entity. In this way each professional understands exactly what he must do.

For example, the masonry worker understands he is to order materials for the foundation concrete, prepare foundation forms, and lay the foundation; he will not paint the bathroom. The electrician is to concern himself only with electrical work; he will not be responsible for a disassociated work unit such as shingling the porch roof.

10.1.2. Segment delineation

Even with a most careful division of a system into separate tasks, there will be some overlap of segments. It will not always be clear which segment encompasses the overlapped work unit. For example, in our house construction effort the frame must be fastened to bolts imbedded in the foundation concrete. It is not clear whether the masonry workers are to set these bolts at the time the foundation is laid, or whether the carpenters are to drive anchor bolts into the hardened concrete at the time the frame is erected. A second example of segment overlap is the holes in wall studs for electrical wiring. Are these holes to be drilled by the carpenters or the electricians?

An effective plan must specify which tasks encompass overlapped work units. For example, a construction plan should declare that masonry workers are to set the frame bolts, or that electricians are to drill wiring holes. Such specification is also required in programming systems. Here a con-

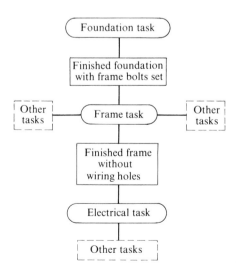

Figure 10.1.

venient form of specification is to declare the inputs to and outputs from each segment. It is then clear exactly what work that segment must do. This could also be done for our construction project.

The inputs to and outputs from the carpentry and electrical segments could be summarized in a block chart, as shown in Fig. 10.1. This block chart shows the flow and interface between tasks. More importantly, it also specifies which tasks encompass the overlapped work units. The chart makes it clear that masonry workers are to set the frame bolts and electricians are to drill the wiring holes.

10.2. Development Plan

Task segmentation provides a basis for the system development plan. It provides a definition point for project manpower allocation and a framework for implementation, and it ensures system modularity.

10.2.1. Manpower allocation

It is both economical and expedient to allocate the implementation effort of a programming project to several members of a programming staff. Two or three experienced analysts can design and organize the system. From this definition point the implementation effort can then be distributed to several less experienced members of the programming staff. The definition point is the system block chart. Each segment of the chart is, in itself, a well-defined task that can be independently presented and allocated to a programming group.

10.2.2. Implementation

The system block chart also forms a framework for implementation. An analysis of system flow with respect to this block chart is used to select implementation techniques. Logical tasks are routed through the chart to assess system bottlenecks and critical processing areas. Programming techniques for each segment are then chosen on the basis of the effects that segment has on overall system efficiency. Critical segments require great care in technique optimization; noncritical segments require less care.

10.2.3. System modularity

A well-defined segmentation of the project effort ensures system modularity. Each task forms a separate, distinct program module. At implementation time each module is developed separately; since the module and its inputs and outputs are well-defined, there is no confusion in the intended interface with other system modules. At checkout time the integrity of the module is tested independently; there are few scheduling problems in synchronizing the completion of several tasks before checkout can begin. Finally, the system is maintained in modular fashion; system errors and deficiencies can be traced to specific system modules, thus limiting the scope of detailed error searching.

10.3. Summary

The system design is the plan for developing a programming system. In this plan the total system effort is divided into smaller tasks or segments, each segment forming a complete logical work unit. In order to delineate the exact extent of a segment, the inputs to and outputs from that segment are declared. The complete system, a composite of all its segments, is then summarized in a system block chart.

The block chart acts as a definition point for system development. From this definition point total system effort may be allocated, by segment, to groups within the programming staff. The processing requirement of the segment has been defined and fixed, as has its interface with other parts of the system. The programming group can approach the segment as a fixed and independent task.

10.4
exercises

(1) What are two basic steps in preparing a system design?

(2) In your own words, define task segmentation.

(3) What must you be careful of in task segmentation?

(4) What is a convenient means of summarizing a programming design?

(5) Of what use is task segmentation in manpower allocation?

(6) Does task segmentation simplify the implementation effort? If so, how?

(7) What is system modularity?

11
sample system design

Let us now return to our compiler system. As groundwork for the design process we will consider the overall processing requirement of the system. This requirement will be formulated as a specific processing philosophy.

11.1. Processing Philosophy

One of two basic processing philosophies may be used for a language processing system, either the direct or the interpretive approach. These two philosophies, or approaches, prescribe the manner in which a system will be fit to the computer. They are basic to the development of the system and must therefore be resolved at an early stage of design.

11.1.1. Direct approach

A language processing system applies, or fits, the commands of a programming language to the computer system. The direct approach is one method by which commands are applied. Commands input to the processing system are translated directly to the machine language of the computer. This machine language is then executed on the computer to carry out the specified transactions or events. For example, a compiler language assignment command $X = Y + 3$ might be translated to three machine commands: LOAD Y (fetch the value of Y), ADD 3 (add 3 to the value of Y), and STORE X (store the result in X). These three machine commands would then carry out the specified assignment when executed on the computer. The direct approach is summarized schematically in Fig. 11.1.

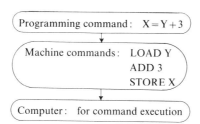

Figure 11.1. Direct approach.

11.1.2 Interpretive approach

On the other hand, an interpretive approach takes a less direct route in fitting the programming language to the computer. Here programming commands are translated to their essence in an intermediate form. An interpreter is then applied to the intermediate forms. As each command is processed the interpreter updates its internal tables in such a manner as to simulate the specified transaction. Figure 11.2 gives a schematic of the interpretive approach.

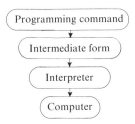

Figure 11.2. Interpretive approach.

11.1.3 Choosing an approach

Each processing approach has its strong and weak points which must be weighed with respect to the language processing system. The direct approach provides faster execution than the interpretive. It produces a machine language program that is submitted, in its entirety, for direct efficient execution on the computer. This has been the approach employed by many batch mode language processing systems.

On the other hand, only an interpretive system can readily interface with an interactive user. As contrasted with the direct approach, the interpreter has complete control over the execution of programming commands. The interpreter drives the processing of a command; the command itself is never given control. It is a simple matter for the interpreter to interface with and respond to an interactive programmer between the interpretation of commands. As a result of this interface the programmer can direct the processing of his programmed commands.

For example, with a compiler system, he could impose breakpoints in statement execution sequence and specify execution starting position. Upon completion of the program segment, selected program variables could be opened for examination. As problem areas are detected in the testing environment the problems would be corrected and testing resumed. In this way the programmer would direct the testing of his program, seeking out and responding to problems in the programmed algorithm.

These considerations in processing philosophy affect the choice of a processing approach for our sample compiler system. Certainly the ideal compiler provides both a direct and an interpretive mode of operation: the interpretive mode for preparation and on-line testing of a programmed algorithm, and the faster direct mode for production and application of the algorithm. For our compiler, however, we will design for and develop only an interpretive operation. This mode of processing satisfies the interactive requirements declared in the system definition.

11.2. Phase Structure

From the statement of processing philosophy we see that our compiler system naturally breaks down into two phases: a parsing phase for accepting programmed commands and converting them to an intermediate form, and an interpretive phase for processing the intermediate forms. These phases appear as shown in Fig. 11.3.

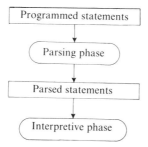

Figure 11.3. Phase structure.

The compiler system operates on a programmed algorithm. Each statement of the algorithm is parsed and converted to intermediate form. Then the interpretive phase is given control to apply the parsed algorithm to the computer. The parsing and interpretive phases represent two complete and distinct stages in the compilation process.

11.3. Phase Delineation

Delineation of the two phases involves fixing the format of parsed statements. The overall content and requirement of each phase is understood. However, it is not clear exactly how they communicate or interface with each other. The parsed statement table is at the crossroads of this interface. It clarifies the direction each phase must take to intersect in a proper and controlled merge.

11.3.1. Parsed statement format

Consideration of overall system efficiency dictates that statements should be parsed to that form most suitable for interpretation. The compiler accepts and parses each statement of a programmed algorithm only once. However, the statement is most probably interpreted many times during execution of the algorithm. The economics of this situation are that any processing work that can be transferred from the interpretive to the parsing phase will increase the efficiency of the total system.

An economically analogous case is that of the fisherman who, at each outing, sounds the river bottom to navigate his way to a known fishing hole. Navigation would be much simpler had he reconstructed the route in the form of a map his first time through. On succeeding trips he could then trace the original route from the map. Our compiler system follows the procedure the fisherman should have used. A statement is processed many times during the handling of a programmed algorithm. When it is first accepted by the system the parser must explore and chart the content of that statement. At this time the statement may be reconstructed in a parsed form. Then, during the interpretive phase, the original exploratory work can be traced, time and again, from the parsed form.

Variable resolution

Part of the required exploratory work is the resolution of program variables. Variables within a programmed algorithm must be recognized and grouped by variable name. At execution time a programmed value is maintained for each variable. The value is the same for variables of the same name. Most of the work in initializing this value structure can be done at parsing time. The work would be summarized in a variable table, and each

Variable name #1	Value entry
Variable name #2	Value entry
. . .	. . .
Variable name #n	Value entry

Figure 11.4. Variable table.

table item would consist of a variable name together with its programmed value (see Fig. 11.4).

Label resolution

In the process of accepting program statements the parser must search for and recognize statement labels. When a label is declared in the programmed algorithm, it is entered into the label table; the entry will contain the label name together with its statement number (see Fig. 11.5). Later on, when that label is referenced in a GO TO LABEL statement, the parser will associate the reference by a pointer into the label table.

Label name # 1	Associated statement number
Label name # 2	Associated statement number
. . .	. . .
Label name # n	Associated statement number

Figure 11.5. Label table.

Parsed statement table

The variable and label tables are aids to act as supplements to the parsed statements of a programmed algorithm. Let us now look at the form of these parsed statements and the table in which they are held.

During the parsing process statements are broken down and converted to an intermediate form. The parser orders statements by statement number and places them in a statement table. The statement table is structured as shown in Fig. 11.6.

1	Parsed form of first statement
2	Parsed form of second statement
	. . .
n	Parsed form of nth statement

Figure 11.6. Statement table.

In the interpretive phase of the compiler this table is used to control the execution of the programmed algorithm; codes and structures within the parsed forms direct the interpretation process. Statement coding procedures are aimed at optimizing interpretation.

To this end all statement forms are coded such that the statement type is immediately available to the interpreter. The first entry in the parsed form will be the type code. Each statement type will have a unique code value: IF, code 0; READ, code 1; PRINT, code 2; ASSIGN, code 3; GO TO, code 4; DO, code 5; END, code 6. Within the parsed statement, label and variable references will be resolved by pointers into the label or variable tables. Boolean and arithmetic expressions are presented in Polish form, with the operators, constants, and variables coded for quick recognition. Finally, a stop code is used to designate the termination of structures and substructures within the parsed form.

The entire coding scheme can be specified in syntax equations. The equations show the parsed structure of specified statement types.

$\langle$parsed statement$\rangle$ :: = $\langle$if clause$\rangle \langle$simple$\rangle$ | $\langle$simple$\rangle$

$\langle$if clause$\rangle$ :: = 0 $\langle$expression$\rangle$

$\langle$simple$\rangle$ :: = $\langle$read$\rangle$ | $\langle$print$\rangle$ | $\langle$assign$\rangle$ | $\langle$go to$\rangle$ | $\langle$do$\rangle$ | $\langle$end$\rangle$

$\langle$read$\rangle$ :: = 1 $\int [\langle$variable$\rangle] \langle$stop$\rangle$

$\langle$print$\rangle$ :: = 2 $\int [\langle$expression$\rangle] \langle$stop$\rangle$

$\langle$assign$\rangle$ :: = 3 $\langle$variable$\rangle \langle$expression$\rangle$

$\langle$go to$\rangle$ :: = 4 $\langle$label table pointer$\rangle$

$\langle$do$\rangle$ :: = 5 $\langle$variable$\rangle \langle$expression$\rangle \langle$expression$\rangle \langle$expression$\rangle$

$\langle$end$\rangle$ :: = 6

$\langle$expression$\rangle$ :: = $\int [\langle$operator$\rangle$ | $\langle$operand$\rangle] \langle$stop$\rangle$

$\langle$operand$\rangle$ :: = $\langle$constant$\rangle$ | $\langle$variable$\rangle$ | $\langle$function$\rangle$

$\langle$constant$\rangle$ :: = 7 $\langle$constant value$\rangle$

$\langle$variable$\rangle$ :: = 8 $\langle$variable table pointer$\rangle$

$\langle$function$\rangle$ :: = $\langle$function code$\rangle \int [\langle$expression$\rangle] \langle$stop$\rangle$

$\langle$function code$\rangle$ :: = $\langle$max$\rangle$ | $\langle$min$\rangle$ | $\langle$abs$\rangle$ | $\langle$sqrt$\rangle$

$\langle$max$\rangle$ :: = 9

$\langle$min$\rangle$ :: = 10

$\langle$abs$\rangle$ :: = 11

$\langle$sqrt$\rangle$ :: = 12

$\langle$operator$\rangle$ :: = $\langle$exponentiate$\rangle$ | $\langle$multiply$\rangle$ | $\langle$divide$\rangle$ | $\langle$subtract$\rangle$ | $\langle$add$\rangle$ |
$\qquad\qquad$ $\langle$equal$\rangle$ | $\langle$unequal$\rangle$ | $\langle$greater$\rangle$ | $\langle$less$\rangle$ | $\langle$greater or equal$\rangle$ |
$\qquad\qquad$ $\langle$less or equal$\rangle$ | $\langle$and$\rangle$ | $\langle$or$\rangle$

$\langle$exponentiate$\rangle$ :: = 13

$\langle$multiply$\rangle$ :: = 14

$\langle$divide$\rangle$ :: = 15

$\langle$subtract$\rangle$ :: = 16

$\langle$add$\rangle$ :: = 17

$\langle$equal$\rangle$ :: = 18

$\langle$unequal$\rangle$ :: = 19

$\langle$greater$\rangle$ :: = 20

$\langle$less$\rangle$ :: = 21

⟨greater or equal⟩ :: = 22
⟨less or equal⟩ :: = 23
⟨and⟩ :: = 24
⟨or⟩ :: = 25
⟨stop⟩ :: = 26

Let us consider a few examples of parsed statement forms. The first example is an assignment statement. The statement together with its parsed form is

Statement
X = 90

Parsed form
3
8
Pointer (X)
7
90
stop

As you can see, the statement is in a most convenient form for interpretation. The code (3) at the beginning of the form immediately designates an assignment statement. Code (8) and Pointer (X) designate the variable to which the assignment is to be made. The interpreter will place the assigned value in the variable table at the position indicated by Pointer. The expression to be assigned contains only a single operand. Code (7) and value (90) indicate that this operand is a constant of value 90. The stop code terminates this expression and the parsed statement.

A facility is present for expressions more complicated than a single operand. Full expressions are represented in Polish forms, with the operators and operands coded for easy recognition. This can be seen in the parsed form of a second assignment statement.

Statement
X = Y + 70

Parsed form

3	Assign
8	
Pointer (X)	X
8	
Pointer (Y)	Y
7	
70	70
17	+
stop	

In this example an assignment is also made to a variable (X). The value assigned is the value of the expression (Y + 70). As an aid to the interpreter in evaluating the expression, the expression is presented in Polish form (Y,70, +). The coding structure makes the operators and operands of the Polish form readily available.

Our coding procedures will support complex programming statements. This is seen in the following example.

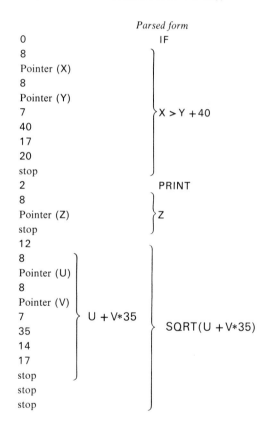

Statement

If X > Y + 40 THEN PRINT(Z,SQRT(U + V*35))

11.3.2. Block chart

We now have a complete description of the parsed statement format, namely, a description of the statement table and its subservient label and variable tables. This description clarifies and pinpoints the processing requirement of the parsing and interpretive phases of the compiler. Parsed statements are the interface and communication between the two phases. Fixing the interface also completes and fixes the interfaced phases. The two phases together with their interface appear in a block chart as shown in Fig. 11.7.

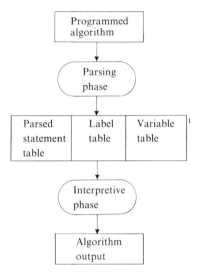

¹ The label and variable tables could be, and usually are, combined in one table.

Figure 11.7. Block chart.

The system is divided into two distinct stages: the parsing phase and the interpretive phase. From this definition point, system development may likewise be split into two stages, each phase developed independently of the other.

11.4. Parsing Phase

Let us consider the parsing phase first. Rather than tackling the complete phase in one approach, this phase can be further divided into two modules.

An acceptance module will be formulated to enter programmed statements from the remote console. This module will be complemented by a parser module for converting the statements to their parsed form.

11.4.1. Acceptance module

A semicolon will be recognized by the acceptance module as a special character that terminates statement text. By use of the semicolon the programmer can enter statements on more than one line of the remote device; he terminates the last line of the statement with a semicolon. For example:

```
GO TO LABEL;
IF  X > Y|X > Z  THEN
DO  I = MIN(Y,Z)  TO  X;
```

The module, when called by the system, forms one statement from the remote console. It returns, as a parameter from the module, the address of that statement. A programmer terminates his algorithm by keying in FINISH. When the acceptance module encounters FINISH it returns a parameter of zero. The module, together with its calling and return parameters, appears as shown in Fig. 11.8.

11.4.2. Parser module

Operating in tandem with the acceptance module is the parser module. The parser module, when called by the system, converts one statement to

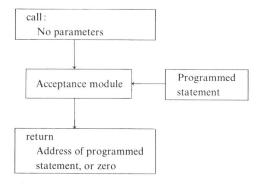

Figure 11.8. Acceptance module.

parsed form and enters that form in the statement table. To do this, it requires as calling parameters the addresses of the programmed statement, the variable table, the label table, and the parsed statement table. It also requires the

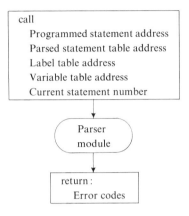

Figure 11.9. Parser module.

current statement number. The module returns an indication of any errors encountered during the parsing process. This indication will be made by an error code parameter. Figure 11.9 outlines the parser module.

11.4.3. Control

Notice that the acceptance and parser modules have been defined as clean logical tasks. The acceptance module accepts one statement; the parser module parses one statement. This precise definition is convenient for allocating the development work for those modules. However, it supports only the processing of one programmed statement, not a complete programmed algorithm.

A control module is required to interface for and direct the flow of acceptance and parsing. Statement by statement a programmed algorithm is accepted and parsed. In case of statement errors, control must request a corrected statement from the interactive user. The control module drives the acceptance and parsing of a programmed algorithm. This module, together with its two slaves, are the composite tasks of the parsing phase. They are summarized in the block chart in Fig. 11.10.

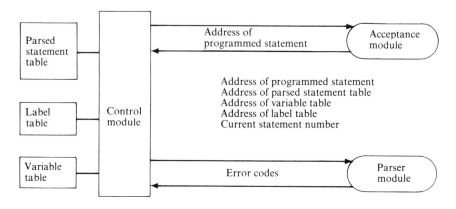

Figure 11.10. Parsing phase.

11.5. Interpretive Phase

The parsing phase prepares a programmed algorithm for interpretation. Let us now look at the interpretive phase. As was the parsing phase, the interpretive phase will be divided into two slave modules and a control module. The primary slave will be the interpreter module.

11.5.1. Interpreter module

When called by the system, the interpreter module will carry out the transactions specified by one statement. Which statement this is, is indicated by a statement number calling parameter. The parsed statement table, label table, and variable table support the interpretive process. Their addresses are also passed as calling parameters. It is the responsibility of the interpreter to maintain instruction execution sequence. When this sequence is altered by GO TO LABEL or DO statements, the interpreter will return the number of the next statement to be executed. The calling and return parameters of the interpreter module are summarized in Fig. 11.11.

11.5.2. Function module

In the process of interpreting statements, functions must be processed and evaluated. When the interpreter encounters a function it will evaluate

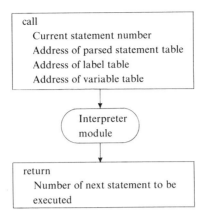

Figure 11.11. Interpreter module.

the function parameters and then request a function value from the function module. The calling parameters to the function module will be function code and function parameter values. Schematically the module appears as shown in Fig. 11.12.

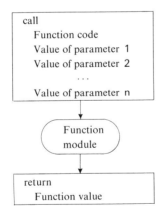

Figure 11.12. Function module.

11.5.3. Control

As stated, the function module is driven by the interpreter module. The interpreter has complete responsibility for the processing of one parsed statement. However, the interpreter, in turn, must be driven through the flow of a programmed algorithm. A control module is defined for this purpose. The control module oversees and directs the interpretation process.

In addition, the control module interfaces with the interactive programmer. Between calls to the interpreter, control will check for and respond to interactive commands. These commands are applied by the control module to the interpretation process.

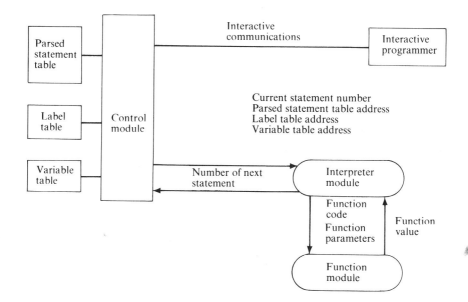

Figure 11.13. Interpretive phase.

The control module completes the interpretive phase. This phase may be summarized in block chart form as shown in Fig. 11.13.

11.6. System Block Chart

The compiler system is a composite of the parsing and interpretive phases. The two phases interface or merge through the statement, label, and variable tables. The complete system is shown schematically in the block chart in Fig. 11.14.

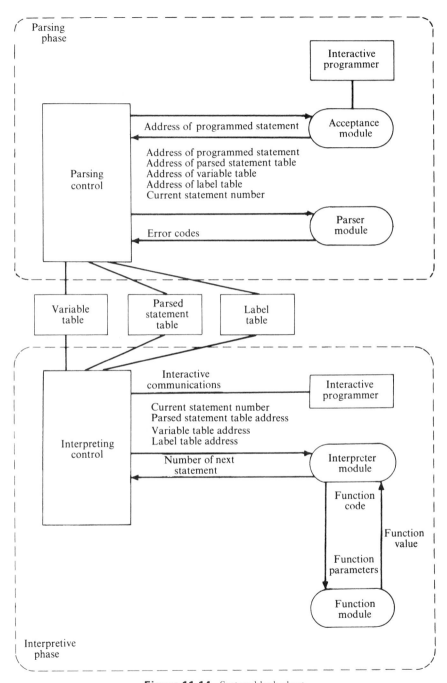

Figure 11.14. System block chart.

11.7. Summary

Design of our compiler has resulted in a plan for system development. In this plan the system was divided into modules; the modules were thoroughly defined. Each was declared from the standpoint of its processing requirement. To clarify and fix this requirement the module inputs (calling parameters) and outputs (return parameters) were fixed. The complete system was then declared as a composite of all its modules; the composite was summarized in a system block chart.

This block chart is to act as a definition point and a plan for a system development. Each module serves as a distinct, independent development task; resolution of all tasks results in resolution of the system. The prescription of each task and its interface is a prescription of the system development plan.

11.8
exercises

(1) What are two goals in designing a language processing system?

(2) What are two processing philosophies for a language processing system?

(3) What reasons should be considered in choosing a philosophy?

(4) What are the two major phases of our compiler system?

(5) What information is carried with each item in the label and variable tables in our system?

(6) What information should be shown in a system block chart?

(7) What is the advantage in converting statements to a coded form?

12
sample system
implementation

In the implementation stage of a system the design plan is carried out. In that plan the total system has been broken into smaller segments. To resolve each of these segments is to implement the total system.

We will approach the implementation of our sample compiler system on a task-segmented basis. The total effort will be segmented into two tasks: implementation of the parsing phase and implementation of the interpretive phase. Effort on these two phases will be further divided into their composite modules. The overall task breakdown appears as follows.

Parsing phase
Acceptance module
Parsing module
Control

Interpretive phase
Interpreter module
Function module
Control

12.1. Parsing Phase

First of the two phases to be implemented will be the parsing phase. Figure
12.1 shows the parsing phase block chart. It serves as a summary of the phase.

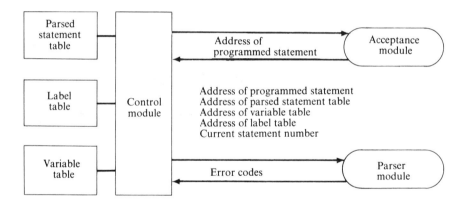

Figure 12.1. Parsing phase block chart.

The phase is divided into three modules: control, acceptance, and
parser. Resolution and implementation of the phase will require the implementation of each of its modules.

12.1.1. Control module

Looking at the block chart, we can see that the phase is driven by a
control module. Each statement of a programmed algorithm is entered into
the computer by the acceptance module and then passed to the parser for

conversion to parsed form. The parsed forms of all statements are to be collected in the parsed statement table; this table is supported by auxiliary label and variable tables.

The control module itself is to do none of the actual work in creating these tables. It will simply direct the two worker modules. As such, the control module requires very little in implementation; only the construction of calling and return parameters for each of its working slaves is necessary.

12.1.2. Acceptance module

As with control, the acceptance module requires very little in implementation. When called it simply accepts the next programmed statement from the remote console.

12.1.3. Parser module

The parser module acts on a statement in its programmed form, converting that statement to parsed form. These forms were declared by syntax equations, which appear as follows. First, we have the programmed statement syntax.

⟨statement⟩ :: = ⟨label⟩ : ⟨command⟩ ; | ⟨command⟩ ;
⟨command⟩ :: = ⟨simple⟩ | ⟨compound⟩
⟨compound⟩ :: = IF ⟨expression⟩ THEN ⟨simple⟩
⟨simple⟩ :: = ⟨read⟩ | ⟨print⟩ | ⟨assign⟩ | ⟨do⟩ | ⟨goto⟩ | ⟨end⟩
⟨read⟩ :: = READ (⟨variable⟩ ∫ [, ⟨variable⟩])
⟨print⟩ :: = PRINT (⟨expression⟩ ∫ [, ⟨expression⟩])
⟨assign⟩ :: = ⟨variable⟩ = ⟨expression⟩
⟨goto⟩ :: = GO TO ⟨label⟩
⟨do⟩ :: = ⟨count⟩ | ⟨index⟩
⟨count⟩ :: = DO ⟨expression⟩ | DO
⟨index⟩ :: = DO ⟨variable⟩ = ⟨expression⟩ TO ⟨expression⟩ BY ⟨expression⟩ |
            DO ⟨variable⟩ = ⟨expression⟩ TO ⟨expression⟩
⟨end⟩ :: = END

⟨expression⟩ :: = ⟨operand⟩ ∫ [⟨infix operator⟩ ⟨operand⟩]
⟨operand⟩ :: = ⟨prefix operator⟩ ⟨prime⟩ | ⟨prime⟩
⟨prime⟩ :: = ⟨constant⟩ | ⟨variable⟩ | ⟨function⟩ | ⟨subexpression⟩
⟨subexpression⟩ :: = (⟨expression⟩)

⟨function⟩ :: = ⟨function name⟩ (⟨expression⟩ ∫ [, ⟨expression⟩]
⟨function name⟩ :: = MIN | MAX | ABS | SQRT
⟨label⟩ :: = ⟨symbol⟩
⟨variable⟩ :: = ⟨symbol⟩
⟨symbol⟩ :: = ⟨alpha⟩ ∫ ⟨alphanumeric⟩
⟨constant⟩ :: = ∫ ⟨numeric⟩
⟨alphanumeric⟩ :: = ⟨alpha⟩ | ⟨numeric⟩
⟨alpha⟩ :: = A | B | C ... | Y | Z
⟨numeric⟩ :: = 1 | 2 | 3 ... | 9 | 0
⟨infix operator⟩ :: = + | − | * | / | ↑ | = | ≠ | < | > | ≤ | ≥
⟨prefix operator⟩ :: = + | −

Second, we have the parsed statement syntax.

⟨parsed statement⟩ :: = ⟨if clause⟩ ⟨simple⟩ | ⟨simple⟩
⟨if clause⟩ :: = 0 ⟨expression⟩
⟨simple⟩ :: = ⟨read⟩ | ⟨print⟩ | ⟨assign⟩ | ⟨go to⟩ | ⟨do⟩ | ⟨end⟩
⟨read⟩ :: = 1 ∫ [⟨variable⟩] ⟨stop⟩
⟨print⟩ :: = 2 ∫ [⟨expression⟩] ⟨stop⟩
⟨assign⟩ :: = 3 ⟨variable⟩ ⟨expression⟩
⟨go to⟩ :: = 4 ⟨label table pointer⟩
⟨do⟩ :: = 5 ⟨variable⟩ ⟨expression⟩ ⟨expression⟩ ⟨expression⟩
⟨end⟩ :: = 6
⟨expression⟩ :: = ∫ [⟨operator⟩ | ⟨operand⟩] ⟨stop
⟨operand⟩ :: = ⟨constant⟩ | ⟨variable⟩ | ⟨function⟩
⟨constant⟩ :: = 7 ⟨constant value⟩
⟨variable⟩ :: = 8 ⟨variable table pointer⟩
⟨function⟩ :: = ⟨function code⟩ ∫ [⟨expression⟩] ⟨stop⟩
⟨function code⟩ :: = ⟨max⟩ | ⟨min⟩ | ⟨abs⟩ | ⟨sqrt⟩
⟨max⟩ :: = 9
⟨min⟩ :: = 10
⟨abs⟩ :: = 11
⟨sqrt⟩ :: = 12
⟨operator⟩ :: = ⟨exponentiate⟩ | ⟨multiply⟩ | ⟨divide⟩ | ⟨subtract⟩ | ⟨add⟩ |
                  ⟨equal⟩ | ⟨unequal⟩ | ⟨greater⟩ | ⟨less⟩ | ⟨greater or equal⟩ |
                  ⟨less or equal⟩ | ⟨and⟩ | ⟨or⟩
⟨exponentiate⟩ :: = 13
⟨multiply⟩ :: = 14
⟨divide⟩ :: = 15
⟨subtract⟩ :: = 16
⟨add⟩ :: = 17
⟨equal⟩ :: = 18

⟨unequal⟩ :: = 19
⟨greater⟩ :: = 20
⟨less⟩ :: = 21
⟨greater or equal⟩ :: = 22
⟨less or equal⟩ :: = 23
⟨and⟩ :: = 24
⟨or⟩ :: = 25
⟨stop⟩ :: = 26

Conversion syntax

To convert from programmed form to parsed form we will create a syntax that combines both formats. The conversion syntax will act on a programmed statement as input and dictate a parsed statement as output.

Let us look in detail at what must be done to convert a statement to its parsed form. An example of such a conversion is the following.

Programmed statement	*Parsed statement*
READ(X,Y)	1
	8
	Variable table pointer (X)
	8
	Variable table pointer (Y)
	stop

The parsed form contains codes to represent items of the programmed form. For example, code (1) designates a READ statement. Each code (8) declares a variable to be read. Code (stop) designates the end of the variable list. The variable codes are supported by pointers to the corresponding variable table entries. The following is the parsed form syntax.

⟨read statement⟩ :: = 1 ⟨variable⟩ ∫ [⟨variable⟩] stop
⟨variable⟩ :: = 8 ⟨variable table pointer⟩

Its counterpart, the programmed form syntax, declares the programmed items which are to bring forth these codes. This syntax appears as follows.

⟨read statement⟩ :: = READ (⟨variable⟩ ∫ [, ⟨variable⟩])
⟨variable⟩ :: = ⟨alpha numeric string⟩

Now we wish to create a conversion syntax that will combine both the programmed and parsed forms. This syntax will declare the form of all programmed items input, together with the parsed items output. Output items will be declared by syntax subroutines. For example, when READ is recognized in the input, an Output(1) subroutine will be declared to output the read statement code; when a variable is detected in the input an output(8) will be specified. To distinguish syntax subroutines from other syntactical entities they will be underlined in the syntax equations. The conversion syntax appears as follows.

⟨read statement⟩ :: = READ (output(1) ⟨variable⟩
                          ∫ [, ⟨variable⟩]) output(stop)
⟨variable⟩ :: = output(8) variable subroutine

The syntax subroutines in these equations perform the following operations.

Output(1) subroutine :   Output code (1)
Output(stop) subroutine : Output code (stop)
Output(8) subroutine :   Output code (8)
Variable subroutine :   Recognize a variable name in the input stream.
                          Resolve that name through the variable table.
                          Output the variable table pointer.

A similar conversion syntax, and supporting syntax subroutines, are created for each type of statement in the programming language. A second example is the PRINT statement, whose conversion syntax is

⟨print statement⟩ :: = PRINT (output(2) ⟨expression⟩
                          ∫ [, ⟨expression⟩]) output(stop)

These are the syntax subroutines.

Output(2) subroutine :   Output code (2)
Output(stop) subroutine : Output code (stop)

When a PRINT is recognized in the input stream, the statement code (2) is output. Each argument of the print list is an expression, to be processed by an ⟨expression⟩ syntax. After the last list item is input, a stop code is output. Naturally the output(stop) subroutine can be the same as the output (stop) subroutine for our previous READ syntax.

To support statement conversion an expression conversion syntax is required. This syntax will transform Boolean and arithmetic expressions into coded Polish form. This, together with the statement syntax, provides a complete conversion structure for our parser module.

Syntax driver

The conversion syntax will be directed on the computer by a syntax driver. The syntax equations, in tabular form, are driven through programmed form to parsed form conversion. Input to the driven syntax is a programmed statement string, outputting a parsed statement string. To maintain position in each of these strings an INPUT CURSOR and OUTPUT CURSOR will be kept.

The driver is constructed in the same manner as that of Chapter 6. To interface with syntax subroutines the driver contains TRUE and FALSE return points. Based on the outcome of a subroutine, it will return either TRUE or FALSE to the driver.

Syntax subroutines

The driver will make the INPUT CURSOR and OUTPUT CURSOR available to syntax subroutines. As a subroutine detects items in the input string or places items in the output string, it will update these cursors. For an example of the use of these cursors recall our conversion syntax for a READ statement.

$$\langle \text{read statement} \rangle :: = \text{READ} (\underline{\text{output(1)}} \langle \text{variable} \rangle$$
$$\int [, \langle \text{variable} \rangle]) \underline{\text{output(stop)}}$$
$$\langle \text{variable} \rangle :: = \underline{\text{output(8) variable subroutine}}$$

The subroutines required for this syntax are

Output(1) subroutine :	Output code (1)
Output(stop) subroutine :	Output code (stop)
Output(8) subroutine :	Output code (8)
Variable subroutine :	Recognize a variable name in the input stream.
	Resolve that name through the variable table.
	Output the variable table pointer.

The output(1), output(stop), and output(8) subroutines may all be combined in an output(X) subroutine. This subroutine will place code (X)

in the output string at position OUTPUT CURSOR. It will then update
the cursor and return TRUE to the syntax driver (Fig. 12.2).

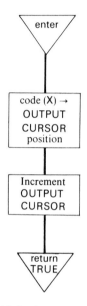

Figure 12.2. Output(X) subroutine.

While output(X) will always return TRUE to the syntax driver, the
variable subroutine will not. The variable subroutine looks for a proper
variable name at a position (INPUT CURSOR) in the input string. If such
a name is found, it is resolved through the variable table, and the variable
table pointer is outputted to the output string. Control is then returned
TRUE to the syntax driver. However, if a variable name is not found in the
input string, the subroutine will return FALSE. The complete subroutine
appears in Fig. 12.3.

The variable and output(X) subroutines are only two examples of the
syntax subroutines we need for our parser module. The points to remember
from their discussion are the interface points with the syntax driver. These
include the INPUT CURSOR and OUTPUT CURSOR; these provide
current positions in the input and output strings. A second type of interface
is the TRUE and FALSE returns to the syntax driver. These returns provide
the driver with information about the success of its current course through
the syntax structure.

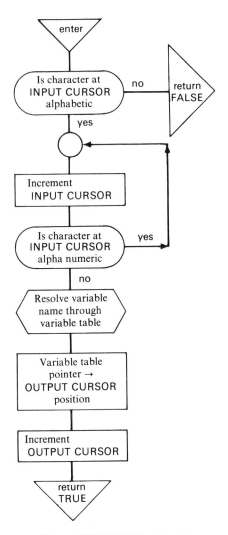

Figure 12.3. Variable subroutine.

Table resolution

Let us now divert attention from syntax directed considerations for a moment to look at table resolution procedures. In Fig. 12.3 there is a processing box entitled "Resolve variable name through variable table." We must now consider just what this resolution involves.

In processing a programmed algorithm the parser builds a variable table. As the algorithm is converted to parsed form, each algorithm variable is identified by a pointer into the variable table. Variables of the same name will point to the same variable table entry. Each entry will carry a variable name together with a position for the variable value. This value does not concern us at the present time; what is of concern is the reference of a parsed algorithm to the variable table. Schematically, this reference can be shown as in Fig. 12.4.

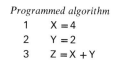

Programmed algorithm

1	X = 4
2	Y = 2
3	Z = X + Y

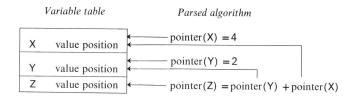

Figure 12.4. Variable table reference.

A programmed algorithm is parsed one statement at a time. When the parser encounters variable (X) in statement 1, it creates an entry for X in the variable table and references this entry by a variable table pointer.

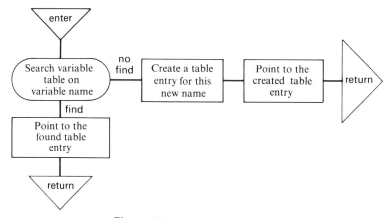

Figure 12.5. Variable resolution.

In statement 2 the parser encounters variable (Y). Another entry is made in the variable table, and that entry is referenced by a pointer. In statement 3 a table entry for variable (Z) is created and referenced. However, when variable (X) and variable (Y) are encountered in statement 3, no variable table entries are created. This is because entries have already been created for these variables in statements 1 and 2. In flow chart form this resolution of a programmed variable appears as shown in Fig. 12.5.

As each variable is encountered the variable table is searched. If a table entry is found for that variable name, then it is the entry to be referenced. If no table entry is found a new table entry is created and referenced.

Label resolution is handled in a manner similar to this. When a labeled statement is encountered by the parser, a label table entry is created for that label name. Associated with the entry is the statement number. For example:

| *Programmed statement* | *Label table entry* |

statement 5   LABEL3:X = Y + Z | LABEL3 | 5 |

Subsequently, when that label is referenced by a GO TO statement, the parser will create a label table pointer. For example:

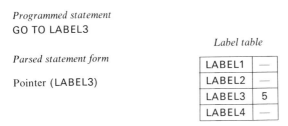

Programmed statement
GO TO LABEL3

Label table

Parsed statement form

Pointer (LABEL3)

LABEL1	—
LABEL2	—
LABEL3	5
LABEL4	—

There is one problem in the above resolution of labels; a label may be referenced before it is declared, as in the following programmed algorithm.

(1)   X = 0
(2)   IF Y > 2 THEN GO TO LABEL1
(3)   X = 1
(4)   LABEL1: PRINT(X)

When this condition, sometimes called a forward reference, occurs, the label must be resolved in reverse order. In statement 2, when the label is

referenced, the parser will create a label table entry with no associated statement number. Subsequently, when the label is declared, the associated
statement number will be filled in.

Two parser subroutines are required to resolve programmed labels:
a label reference and a label declaration subroutine. Each must search the
label table for an existing same name entry. If no such entry exists, a new
entry will be created. The label declaration subroutine will associate a
statement number with the label table entry; the label reference subroutine
will create a pointer to that entry. In flow chart form, these subroutines
appear as shown in Fig. 12.6.

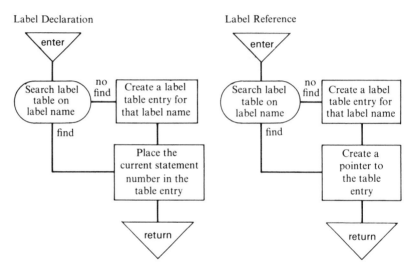

Figure 12.6. Label subroutines.

Table search structures

As you can see, both variable and label resolutions require a search
and insert mechanism. This mechanism is of considerable consequence in
the execution efficiency of a parsing algorithm.

In complexity the syntax driver and syntax equations take up the bulk
of a parsing algorithm. However, when the algorithm is executed, the
symbol search mechanisms take the bulk of the execution time. It is quite
surprising to observe the speed and efficiency with which a syntax driver
will step through a complicated syntax structure in processing programmed
statements. Although the process is logically complex, it requires relatively

little computing time. On the other hand, the resolution of programmed symbols requires a great deal of computing time. At each occurrence of a programmed symbol, the symbol table must be searched for its resolution.

A sophisticated search structure could therefore be suggested for the symbol table. For our compiler system we will choose a balanced binary tree search structure. This choice provides a well-rounded approach to the resolution of labels and variables. \

Syntax direction

Recall that resolution of labels and variables is concerned with the label and variable syntax subroutines. Let us now return to the general topics of syntax and of syntax direction.

We talked briefly of the syntax equations for our parser module. In that discussion we considered specific examples of a conversion syntax for READ and PRINT statements. The syntax combined both the programmed and parsed syntactical forms. It appeared as follows.

$$\langle \text{read statement} \rangle :: = \text{READ} (\underline{\text{output(1)}} \langle \text{variable} \rangle$$
$$\int [, \langle \text{variable} \rangle]) \underline{\text{output(stop)}}$$
$$\langle \text{print statement} \rangle :: = \text{PRINT} (\underline{\text{output(2)}} \langle \text{expression} \rangle$$
$$\int [, \langle \text{expression} \rangle]) \underline{\text{output(stop)}}$$

We will now continue this discussion and formulate the complete conversion syntax for the parser. It will accept as input one programmed statement and produce as output the parsed form of that statement. These forms appear in syntax equations as follows.

$\langle \text{statement} \rangle :: = \underline{\text{label declaration}} : \langle \text{command} \rangle ; | \langle \text{command} \rangle ;$
$\langle \text{command} \rangle :: = \langle \text{if clause} \rangle \langle \text{simple} \rangle | \langle \text{simple} \rangle$
$\langle \text{if clause} \rangle :: = \underline{\text{output(0)}} \langle \text{expression} \rangle$
$\langle \text{simple} \rangle :: = \langle \text{read} \rangle | \langle \text{print} \rangle | \langle \text{assign} \rangle | \langle \text{go to} \rangle | \langle \text{do} \rangle | \langle \text{end} \rangle$
$\langle \text{read} \rangle :: = \text{READ} (\underline{\text{output(1)}} \langle \text{variable} \rangle \int [, \langle \text{variable} \rangle]) \underline{\text{output(stop)}}$
$\langle \text{print} \rangle :: = \text{PRINT} (\underline{\text{output(2)}} \langle \text{expression} \rangle \int [, \langle \text{expression} \rangle]) \underline{\text{output(stop)}}$
$\langle \text{assign} \rangle :: = \underline{\text{output(3)}} \langle \text{variable} \rangle = \langle \text{expression} \rangle$
$\langle \text{go to} \rangle :: = \text{GO TO} \underline{\text{output(4)} \text{ label reference}}$
$\langle \text{do} \rangle :: = \text{DO} \underline{\text{output(5)}} \langle \text{do body} \rangle$
$\langle \text{do body} \rangle :: = \langle \text{index} \rangle | \langle \text{count} \rangle$
$\langle \text{index} \rangle :: = \langle \text{variable} \rangle = \langle \text{expression} \rangle \text{ TO} \langle \text{expression} \rangle \langle \text{increment} \rangle$
$\langle \text{increment} \rangle :: = \text{BY} \langle \text{expression} \rangle | \langle \text{express1} \rangle$

⟨count⟩ :: = ⟨dummy variable⟩⟨express1⟩⟨iterations⟩
⟨iterations⟩ :: = ⟨expression⟩⟨express1⟩ | ⟨express1⟩⟨express1⟩
⟨end⟩ :: = END output(6)

In this syntax, syntax subroutines are used to place codes and indicators in the output string. The already familiar output(X) subroutine is used to output statement codes and stop codes. A label declaration and label reference subroutine are used to resolve programmed labels.

Notice the division of a DO statement into two forms: ⟨index⟩ and ⟨count⟩. Let us look first at the ⟨index⟩ form. Two programmed examples of this form are

DO I = 1 TO N BY 2
DO I = 1 TO N

In the first of these examples the increment value (BY 2) is declared. In the second example the increment value is not declared; it is to receive the default value (BY 1). The increment value, or its default, is handled by the ⟨increment⟩ equation. If the value is present it is processed as an ⟨expression⟩; if it is not present a default value is output by the call to ⟨express1⟩.

A second form of the DO statement is the ⟨count⟩ form. Programmed examples of this are

DO 8
DO

In the first example an iteration count of 8 is specified. In the second example the count is not specified; it is to receive a default count of 1. In either case a dummy index variable is created. It is to receive an initial value of 1 and an increment value of 1. For example:

DO N → DO DUMMYVARIABLE = 1 TO N BY 1
DO   → DO DUMMYVARIABLE = 1 TO 1 BY 1

All of these default forms are produced by the ⟨dummy variable⟩ and ⟨express1⟩ calls in the ⟨count⟩ and ⟨iterations⟩ syntax equations.

The statement syntax declares the input and output forms of programmed statements. To support this syntax an ⟨expression⟩ syntax is

required. It will convert a programmed expression to coded Polish form in
the same manner as described in Chapter 5.

⟨expression⟩ :: = ⟨priority 5⟩ ∫ [& ⟨priority 5⟩ output(24) |
                    "|" ⟨priority 5⟩ output(25)] output(stop)
⟨priority 5⟩ :: = ⟨priority 4⟩ ∫ [= ⟨priority 4⟩ output(18) |
                    ≠ ⟨priority 4⟩ output(19) |
                    > ⟨priority 4⟩ output(20) |
                    < ⟨priority 4⟩ output(21) |
                    ≥ ⟨priority 4⟩ output(22) |
                    ≤ ⟨priority 4⟩ output(23)]
⟨priority 4⟩ :: = ⟨priority 3⟩ ∫ [− ⟨priority 3⟩ output(16) |
                    + ⟨priority 3⟩ output(17)]
⟨priority 3⟩ :: = ⟨priority 2⟩ ∫ [* ⟨priority 2⟩ output(14) |
                    / ⟨priority 2⟩ output(15)]
⟨priority 2⟩ :: = ⟨priority 1⟩ ∫ [↑ ⟨priority 1⟩ output(13)]
⟨priority 1⟩ :: = − ⟨constant 0⟩ ⟨operand⟩ output(16) |
                    + ⟨operand⟩ | ⟨operand⟩
⟨operand⟩ :: = ⟨constant⟩ | ⟨variable⟩ | ⟨function⟩ | ⟨subexpression⟩
⟨subexpression⟩ :: = (⟨expression⟩)

The output(X) subroutines in these equations output the proper
codes for expression operators. A completed expression is terminated by
output(stop).

Notice the call to ⟨constant 0⟩ in equation ⟨priority 1⟩. It is used to
convert a prefix minus to subtraction. This is done as follows: an expression (−X) is treated as though it were written (O −X). When the
prefix minus is encountered, a constant (O) is output before operand (X),
and a subtraction operator is output after operand (X). While the
⟨constant 0⟩ call is required for processing infix minus, it is not required
for infix plus. An infix plus, encountered in the input stream, is simply
ignored. This is also seen in equation ⟨priority 1⟩.

The syntax equations for expressions declare the input and output forms
of the basic entities of a programmed expression. However, they must be
supported by a syntax of the basic entities themselves. These include
functions, constants, and variables. Their syntax appears as follows.

⟨function⟩ :: = MAX output(9) ⟨argument list⟩ |
                MIN output(10) ⟨argument list⟩ |
                ABS output(11) ⟨argument⟩ |
                SQRT output(12) ⟨argument⟩

⟨argument list⟩ :: = (⟨expression⟩ ∫ [, ⟨expression ⟩]) output(stop)
⟨argument⟩ :: = (⟨expression⟩) output(stop)
⟨constant⟩ :: = output(7) constant subroutine
⟨variable⟩ :: = output(8) variable subroutine
⟨dummy variable⟩ :: = output(8) dummy variable subroutine
⟨express1⟩ :: = ⟨constant1⟩ output(stop)
⟨constant0⟩ :: = output(7) constant value 0
⟨constant1⟩ :: = output(7) constant value 1

Again the output(X) subroutines are used to output appropriate code
values. These are augmented by constant, variable, and dummy variable
subroutines for the resolution and output of programmed constants and
variables, and by constant value subroutines to output default constant
values.

Combining this syntax with the statement and expression syntax, we
have a complete conversion syntax for our parser module. It appears in
total as follows. First, we have the statement syntax.

⟨statement⟩ :: = label declaration : ⟨command⟩ ; | ⟨command⟩ ;
⟨command⟩ :: = ⟨if clause⟩ ⟨simple⟩ | ⟨simple⟩
⟨if clause⟩ :: = output(0) ⟨expression⟩
⟨simple⟩ :: = ⟨read⟩ | ⟨print⟩ | ⟨assign⟩ | ⟨go to⟩ | ⟨do⟩ | ⟨end⟩
⟨read⟩ :: = READ (output(1) ⟨variable⟩ ∫ [, ⟨variable⟩]) output(stop)
⟨print⟩ :: = PRINT (output(2) ⟨expression⟨ ∫ [, ⟨expression⟩]) output(stop)
⟨assign⟩ :: = output(3) ⟨variable⟩ = ⟨expression⟩
⟨go to⟩ :: = GO TO output(4) label reference
⟨do⟩ :: = DO output(5) ⟨do body⟩
⟨do body⟩ :: = ⟨index⟩ | ⟨count⟩
⟨index⟩ :: = ⟨variable⟩ = ⟨expression⟩ TO ⟨expression⟩ ⟨increment⟩
⟨increment⟩ :: = BY ⟨expression⟩ | ⟨express1⟩
⟨count⟩ :: = ⟨dummy variable⟩ ⟨express1⟩ ⟨iterations⟩
⟨iterations⟩ :: = ⟨expression⟩ ⟨express1⟩ | ⟨express1⟩ ⟨express1⟩
⟨end⟩ :: = END output(6)

Second, there is the expression syntax.

⟨expression⟩ :: = ⟨priority 5⟩ ∫ [& ⟨priority 5⟩ output(24) |
                "|" ⟨priority 5⟩ output(25)] output(stop)
⟨priority 5⟩ :: = ⟨priority 4⟩ ∫ [= ⟨priority 4⟩ output(18)
                ≠ ⟨priority 4⟩ output(19) |
                > ⟨priority 4⟩ output(20) |

$$< \langle \text{priority 4} \rangle \ \underline{\text{output(21)}} \ |$$
$$\geq \langle \text{priority 4} \rangle \ \underline{\text{output(22)}} \ |$$
$$\leq \langle \text{priority 4} \rangle \ \underline{\text{output(23)}} \ ]$$
$$\langle \text{priority 4} \rangle \ ::= \langle \text{priority 3} \rangle \int [\ - \langle \text{priority 3} \rangle \ \underline{\text{output(16)}} \ |$$
$$+ \langle \text{priority 3} \rangle \ \underline{\text{output(17)}} \ ]$$
$$\langle \text{priority 3} \rangle \ ::= \langle \text{priority 2} \rangle \int [* \langle \text{priority 2} \rangle \ \underline{\text{output(14)}} \ |$$
$$/ \langle \text{priority 2} \rangle \ \underline{\text{output(15)}} \ ]$$
$$\langle \text{priority 2} \rangle \ ::= \langle \text{priority 1} \rangle \int [\ \uparrow \ \langle \text{priority 1} \rangle \ \underline{\text{output(13)}} \ ]$$
$$\langle \text{priority 1} \rangle \ ::= \ - \langle \text{constant 0} \rangle \ \langle \text{operand} \rangle \ \underline{\text{output(16)}} \ |$$
$$+ \langle \text{operand} \rangle \ | \ \langle \text{operand} \rangle$$
$$\langle \text{operand} \rangle \ ::= \langle \text{constant} \rangle \ | \ \langle \text{variable} \rangle \ | \ \langle \text{function} \rangle \ | \ \langle \text{subexpression} \rangle$$
$$\langle \text{subexpression} \rangle \ ::= (\ \langle \text{expression} \rangle \ )$$

Third, there is the function, constant, and variable syntax.

$$\langle \text{function} \rangle \ ::= \text{MAX} \ \underline{\text{output(9)}} \ \langle \text{argument list} \rangle \ |$$
$$\text{MIN} \ \underline{\text{output(10)}} \ \langle \text{argument list} \rangle \ |$$
$$\text{ABS} \ \underline{\text{output(11)}} \ \langle \text{argument} \rangle \ |$$
$$\text{SQRT} \ \underline{\text{output(12)}} \ \langle \text{argument} \rangle$$
$$\langle \text{argument list} \rangle \ ::= (\ \langle \text{expression} \rangle \int [, \ \langle \text{expression} \rangle \ ] \ ) \ \underline{\text{output(stop)}}$$
$$\langle \text{argument} \rangle \ ::= (\ \langle \text{expression} \rangle \ ) \ \underline{\text{output(stop)}}$$
$$\langle \text{constant} \rangle \ ::= \underline{\text{output(7)}} \ \underline{\text{constant subroutine}}$$
$$\langle \text{variable} \rangle \ ::= \underline{\text{output(8)}} \ \underline{\text{variable subroutine}}$$
$$\langle \text{dummy variable} \rangle \ ::= \underline{\text{output(8)}} \ \underline{\text{dummy variable subroutine}}$$
$$\langle \text{express1} \rangle \ ::= \langle \text{constant1} \rangle \ \underline{\text{output(stop)}}$$
$$\langle \text{constant0} \rangle \ ::= \underline{\text{output(7)}} \ \underline{\text{constant value 0}}$$
$$\langle \text{constant1} \rangle \ ::= \underline{\text{output(7)}} \ \underline{\text{constant value 1}}$$

The subroutines required to support this syntax are

constant subroutine: Accept a numeric constant from the input and output the constant value.

constant value X: Output constant value (X).

dummy variable subroutine: Create a dummy variable table entry and output a pointer to that entry.

label declaration: Accept an alphanumeric label name from the input and resolve that name through the label table.

label reference: Accept an alphanumeric label name from the input, resolve this name through the label table, and output the label table pointer.

output(**X**):   Output code (**X**).

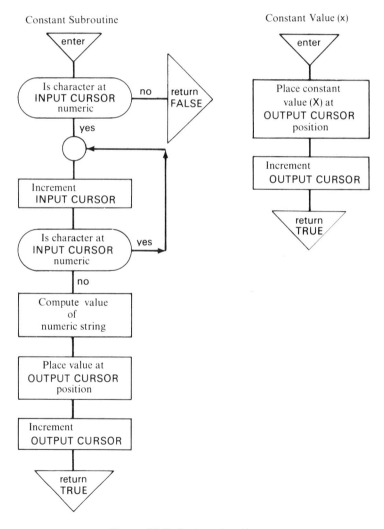

Figure 12.7. Syntax subroutines.

variable subroutine: Accept an alphanumeric variable name from the
input, resolve that name through the variable table, and output
the variable table pointer.

These subroutines may be precisely expressed in flow chart form as
shown in Fig. 12.7.

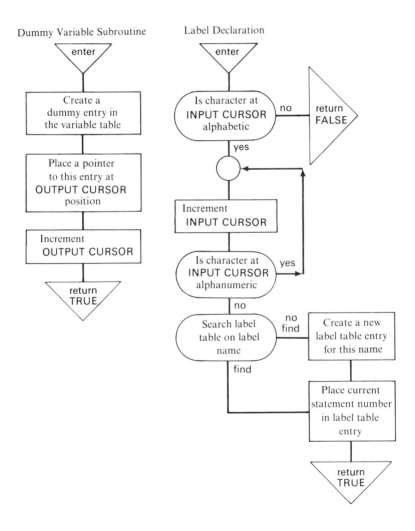

Figure 12.7. Syntax subroutines—(continued).

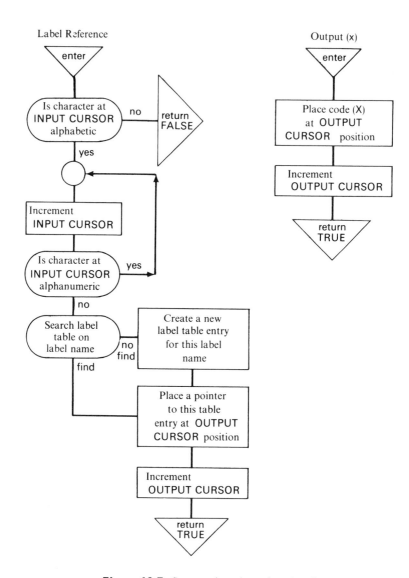

Figure 12.7. Syntax subroutines—(continued).

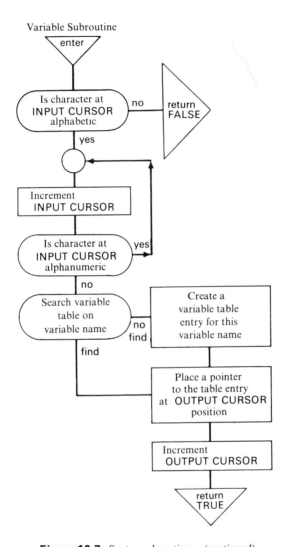

Figure 12.7. Syntax subroutines—(continued).

These subroutines operate in conjunction with the syntax equations and syntax driver. The driver will step through a tabular form of the syntax equations, directing the conversion process. As syntax subroutine calls are encountered in the equation tables, the appropriate subroutine will be activated. This interface of driver to syntax equations to syntax sub-routines may be shown in block chart form; the block chart in Fig. 12.8 is a complete schematic of our parser module.

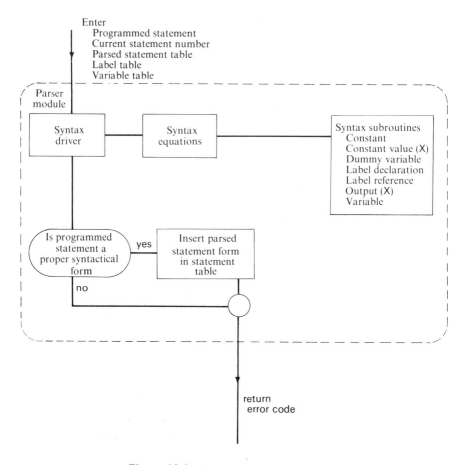

Figure 12.8. Parser module block chart.

Error diagnostics

As shown in the block chart in Fig. 12.8, the parser module returns an error code to the system. This code is an indication of the presence, or absence, of errors occurring during the parsing process. These include errors such as statement table overflow, variable table overflow, label table overflow, syntax driver stack table overflow, and duplicate label declaration.

These errors are quite easily diagnosed by the parser. The first four are simple table overflow conditions. All tables of a system should be supported by overflow tests; when an overflow condition arises, the condition ought to be diagnosed and reported. The fifth diagnostic is for duplicate labels. If two statements of a programmed algorithm are prefixed by the same label, the second label declaration should be diagnosed as a duplicate. This is done easily in the label subroutine.

Also of interest are the syntax errors. There should be a provision to detect and diagnose punctuation errors, misspellings, illegal constructions, etc. in a programmed statement. These may all be grouped in the syntax error category. When such an error occurs, it is helpful to report not only its occurrence, but also the position where it occurred in the statement. For example:

```
IF  HEIGHT +WIDTH >MAX  THEN  VOLUME = MIN)  100, LENGTH*10)
 *** SYNTAX ERROR BEGINNING WITH TEXT ")100,LENGTH*10)"
```

Such an error diagnosis can be made quite simply in the syntax driver. To see this, let us consider the basics of our syntax driven module. The driver maintains an INPUT CURSOR position on the programmed statement throughout the parsing process. As structures in the statement are recognized by the driven syntax, this cursor is advanced. However, the driver will not be able to push the INPUT CURSOR past an error position in the programmed statement. The point of this discussion is that the INPUT CURSOR will be advanced to, but never past, an error position.

The syntax driver can then keep track of the highest position reached by the INPUT CURSOR during the parsing of a statement. If the statement is proven in error by the driven syntax, the highest INPUT CURSOR position will be the precise position of error in the statement. As an aid to the interactive programmer, the system can then report a small section of statement text beginning at this position.

Another type of error condition that should be diagnosed is program sequence errors. The system should check to see that a programmed algorithm is formed from a proper sequence of programmed statements. In our compiler system, this means that DO and END statements should be properly matched. For each DO there must be a mated END, for each END a mated DO. Examples of proper and improper DO-END sequences are as follows.

Proper	*Proper*	*Improper*	*Improper*
DO	DO	DO	DO
DO	DO	DO	DO
END	DO	END	END
END	END		END
	END		END
	END		

To check for proper program sequence the parser module will keep a DO sequence count. Whenever a DO statement is encountered, this count will be incremented. It will be decremented for an END statement. This count will be tested as follows. If the count ever goes negative an unmated END statement has been processed. If, at the completion of the algorithm, the count is nonzero, then one or more END statements are missing. These error conditions will be diagnosed and reported by the parser module.

Proper diagnosis and reporting of programmed error conditions are important in a language processing system. Being only human, the programmer will make mistakes in using the system. He can use diagnosis and instruction from the system to recover from and correct his own programmed errors.

Parsing phase summary

Error diagnostics are but one portion of a module in the parsing phase. Let us now return to the overall processing of this phase. The parsing phase acts on programmed statements, converting those statements to parsed form. In their parsed form the statements are held in a parsed statement

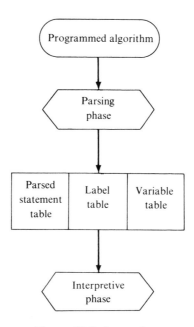

Figure 12.9. System flow.

table, which is supported by auxiliary label and variable tables. After processing the last statement of a programmed algorithm, the parser passes these tables on to the interpretive phase for execution of the algorithm. In block chart form the overall processing flow appears as shown in Fig. 12.9.

12.2. Interpretive Phase

We have shown the implementation of and flow for the parsing phase. Let us now turn to the second phase of our compiler system: the interpretive phase. As ground work for its development recall the interpretive phase block chart (see Fig. 12.10).

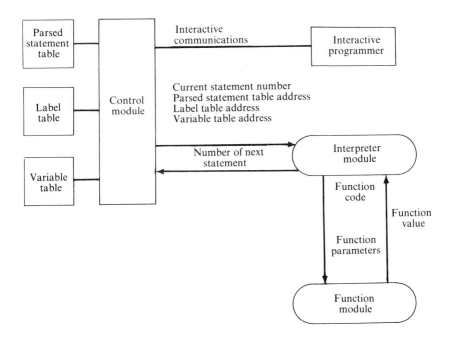

Figure 12.10. Interpretive phase block chart.

From this chart we see that the interpretive phase is divided into three modules: control, interpreter, and function modules. Of these modules we will look at control first.

12.2.1. Control

We feel the complete details of the interface between the control module and the interactive programmer are somewhat far afield from the prime subject of the book. We will therefore only briefly discuss the role of the control module.

The control module drives the interpreter and its slave function module. Control simply acts as a focal point for interpretation of a programmed algorithm. In the actual processing of the algorithm the control module does little work. It simply repeatedly calls the interpreter module to carry out the execution of each successive statement in the algorithm. The real task of the control module is to interface with the interactive programmer. It must respond to the direction of the programmer in controlling the testing of his algorithm.

12.2.2. Function module

Recalling again the interpretive phase block chart of Fig. 12.10, we see that the phase also contains a function module. The control module drives an interpreter, which in turn drives the function module. As with the control

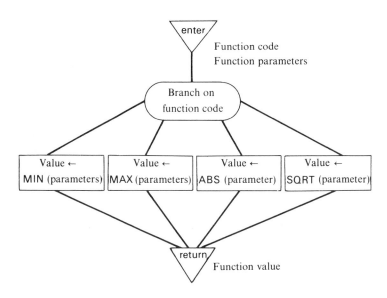

Figure 12.11. Function module.

module, this function module is somewhat unsophisticated in its support of the total interpretive process.

When called, the function module receives the function code together with the numeric value of each function parameter. The module computes the value of this function and returns the value to the system. In flow chart form the module appears simply as shown in Fig. 12.11.

12.2.3. Interpreter module

The workhorse of the interpretive phase is the interpreter module. As you will recall from the phase block chart, the interpreter module is to carry out the execution of a single parsed statement. According to the current statement number, it locates the parsed, coded form of that statement in the statement table. It then scans this coded form, responding to and carrying out the coded transactions.

In doing this, the interpreter must keep track of where it is in the coded statement. To this end a STATEMENT CURSOR will be maintained which points to the current statement position (see Fig. 12.12). As codes within the statement are processed, the cursor is advanced to the next coded transaction.

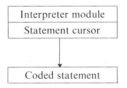

Figure 12.12.

There is a natural division of statement processing into the different statement types. The processing of a GO TO statement requires different computing algorithms than does a DO or PRINT statement. Our interpreter module is divided along these lines. It consists of a subroutine for each type of statement and a driver to control these subroutines. Several of the statement subroutines must process and evaluate programmed expressions. To support these we must also create an expression subroutine. Expressions of a statement will be evaluated through this common subroutine. In block chart form our module is structured as shown in Fig. 12.13.

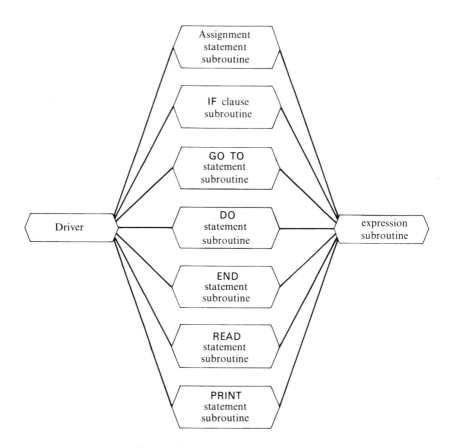

Figure 12.13. Interpreter structure.

12.2.4. Driver subroutine

The function of the interpreter driver is to initialize the module for processing a coded statement. It positions the STATEMENT CURSOR at the beginning of the statement and activates the appropriate statement subroutine. It also initializes the setting of the next sequential statement.

The interpreter module is responsible for maintaining the flow of execution through a programmed algorithm. As each statement is processed, the statement to be processed next must be determined. For several statements (ASSIGN, READ, and PRINT), NEXT STATEMENT will always be the next sequential statement of the programmed algorithm. For other statements (GO TO, DO, and END), this sequence may be altered. Before activating the current statement subroutine the driver will set NEXT STATEMENT to the next sequential statement. In case this sequence is altered by a GO TO, DO, or END, the alteration to NEXT STATEMENT will be made by the statement subroutine. In flow chart form our driver appears as shown in Fig. 12.14.

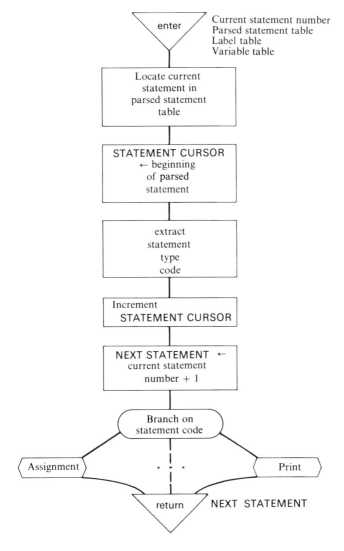

Figure 12.14. Interpreter driver.

12.2.5. Statement subroutines

Let us now look at the subroutines called by the interpreter driver. The statement subroutines are called with the STATEMENT CURSOR pointing at the coded statement text. Throughout the processing of the statement, this cursor will be updated and positioned in the statement.

The variable table is available to the subroutines for extracting and assigning program values. The label table is available for resolving label references. The expression subroutine is available for resolving and evaluating statement expressions.

Let us consider the assignment statement subroutine. An assignment statement in its programmed and parsed form appears as follows.

Programmed form	*Parsed form*
X = Y + 71	3
STATEMENT CURSOR→8	
	Variable table pointer (X)
	8
	Variable table pointer (Y)
	7
	71
	17
	stop

The programmed statement specifies the assignment of an expression (Y + 71) to variable (X). When the statement subroutine is called, STATEMENT CURSOR is positioned as indicated above. The subroutine saves the variable table pointer for X, calls EXPRESSION to compute the value of (Y + 71), and places this value in the variable table entry for X. In flow chart form this appears as shown in Fig. 12.15.

The READ and PRINT statement subroutines are equally straightforward in implementation. The READ statement, for example, READ(X,Y), enters a list of values and assigns them to specified program variables. The PRINT statement, for example, PRINT(Y + 2,SQRT(X)), prints a list of expression values. In each case the parsed statement form contains a stop code to terminate the read/print list. The subroutines scan the coded forms on STATEMENT CURSOR, reading/printing list values, until the stop code is encountered. In flow chart form they appear as shown in Fig. 12.16.

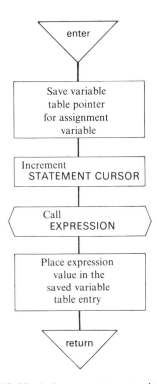

Figure 12.15. Assignment statement subroutine.

Any of the statements may be prefixed by an IF CLAUSE. If the clause (expression) is true, then the statement will be executed; otherwise it will not be. For example, IF A > B THEN PRINT(C) prints C if, and only if, A is larger than B. The subroutine to handle an IF CLAUSE appears as shown in Fig. 12.17.

The GO TO statement alters the flow of statement execution in a programmed algorithm. For example, GO TO LABEL1 specifies that the statement at LABEL1 is to be executed next. In the parsed form of a GO TO statement there is a pointer to the label table entry for the declared label name. There in the label table, the statement number carrying that label is held. Our GO TO statement subroutine fetches this statement number and places the number in NEXT STATEMENT. Figure 12.18 shows the flow chart for the GO TO statement subroutine.

All of the previous statement subroutines were simple and straightforward. They are to be contrasted with the DO-END subroutines, which

Read Statement Subroutine   Print Statement Subroutine

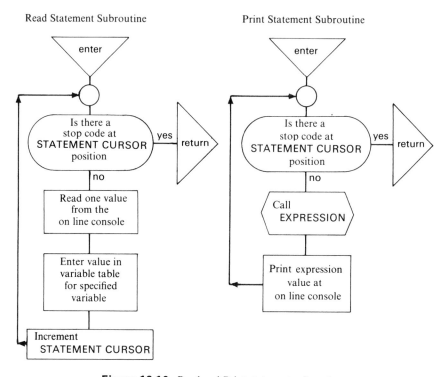

Figure 12.16. Read and Print statement subroutines.

are a little more involved. As an introduction to this topic we will consider the general form of a DO-END structure.

The structure controls the execution of statements within the DO range. For example:

$$DO\ I = 1\ TO\ N\ BY\ 2$$
$$X = X + I$$
$$END$$

This structure forms the sum $(1 + 3 + 5 + 7 + \ldots + N)$. The DO range houses a single statement $(X = X + I)$. Execution of this statement is controlled by the DO and END. An *index variable* (I) is basic to the control. I is assigned an *initial value* (1). At each iteration of the DO range the index variable is updated by an *increment value* (2). Iteration continues until the index variable reaches its *final value* (N). At that time the final iteration of the DO range is processed, and execution drops down through the END statement.

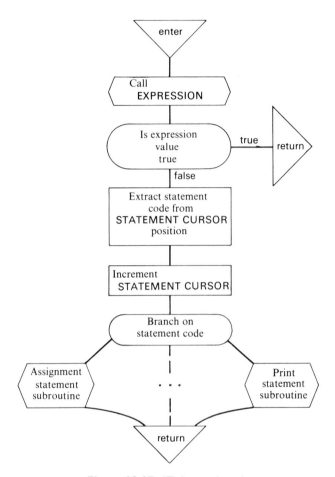

Figure 12.17. IF clause subroutine.

The DO statement subroutine processes a DO statement from its parsed form. In this form the index variable, initial value, increment value, and final value are readily available to the subroutine. In fact, we could show the parsed form as a schematic composite of these four items.

Programmed form
DO I = 1 TO N BY 2

Schematic parsed form
Index variable (I)
Initial value (1)
Final value (N)
Increment value (2)

Figure 12.18. GO TO statement subroutine.

When processing a DO structure, the DO statement subroutine will initialize and save these four items; the END statement subroutine will subsequently examine those items to see if iteration is to continue. This processing flow can be shown schematically as follows.

DO statement: Save index variable, initial value, final value, and increment value
DO range
END statement: Test these values to see if iteration is to be continued

Because our compiler supports nested DO loops, there is a requirement on the way these items are to be saved. Consider, for a moment, the following example of a nested DO structure.

```
DO I = 1 TO N BY 2
    X = X + I
    DO J = 2 TO M BY 1 ⎱
        Y = Y + I*J      ⎰ DO range 1 ⎱ DO range 2
    END                              ⎰
END
```

In processing this structure our DO subroutine would have to save the values for two index variables (I and J). The END statement subroutine would then have to select one of these index values to look at; it would also have to select a DO range to iterate over.

To resolve these selections all index variable values will be held in a stack table. As each DO statement is encountered a new set of values will be stacked. When the mated END is encountered the values are unstacked and examined. Associated with each set of values will be the statement number of the associated DO range. In rough flow chart form our DO-END processing appears as shown in Fig. 12.19.

Let us now expand this DO-END processing approach to fit our interpreter module. Within the module, STATEMENT CURSOR must be maintained, the EXPRESSION subroutine will be called to calculate the index variable values, and finally NEXT STATEMENT will be set to reiterate DO range statements. Formulated as a DO statement subroutine and END statement subroutine for our interpreter module, this approach appears as shown in Fig. 12.20.

12.2.6. Expression subroutine

The above subroutines are but two of seven statement subroutines of the interpreter module. Each statement subroutine must act on a parsed form, processing and evaluating expressions as the parsed form dictates. To support these statement subroutines we will create an expression subroutine. All expressions will be processed through this common subroutine.

---

[1] This is a simple means of processing nested DO-END structures. As such it carries with it certain restrictions. These restrictions are

(1) Unconditional first iteration: The DO range will always be executed at least once. There is no test for completion before beginning the first iteration.

(2) GO TO restriction: GO TO statements that pass control out of the DO range will not be permitted. At each such occurrence of a GO TO statement, a stack entry will be left in the stack table. Eventually the table will fill, and processing will be forced to terminate.

There are ways to avoid both of these restrictions. One such way is to use a DO-END stack at parsing time. Through this stack the statement number of each DO can be placed in the parsed form of its mated END, and the number of each END can be placed in its mated DO. Then at execution time the stack table can be discarded. At each DO statement the index variable is tested for termination, before the first iteration. At each END statement the mated DO is scanned to reconstruct the index variable values.

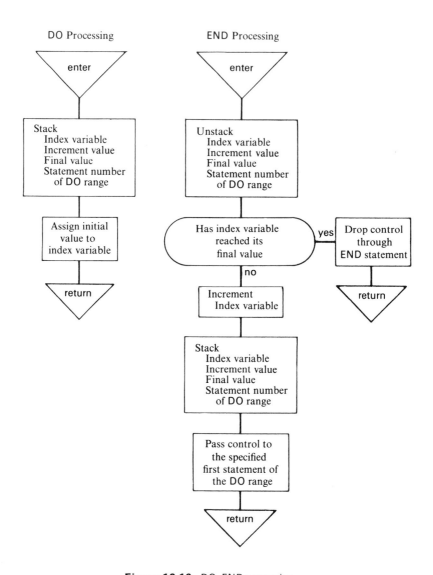

Figure 12.19. DO-END processing.

The expression subroutine maintains its position in the parsed expression as the expression is scanned. It is called with STATEMENT CURSOR pointing to the beginning of the expression text. As items of the expression are processed, STATEMENT CURSOR will be advanced, until at completion of the expression STATEMENT CURSOR will point

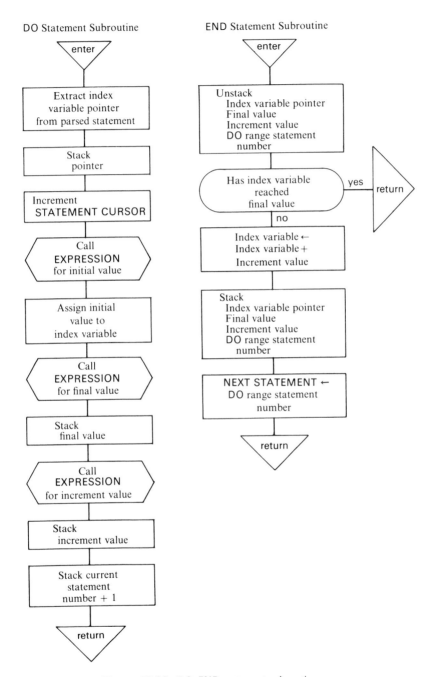

Figure 12.20. DO-END statement subroutines.

to the end of the string. Thus, when the subroutine is excited the cursor will be available for use elsewhere in the program.

To see how the subroutine is called, consider an expression and its parsed form.

Expression

70*(X + 100)

Parsed form

STATEMENT CURSOR 7
                       70 } 70

                       8
              Pointer (X) } X

                       7
                      100 } 100

                      17   +
                      14   *
                    stop

As shown, STATEMENT CURSOR will point to the beginning of the parsed form when the expression subroutine is called. The parsed form will be presented in Polish.

The subroutine will evaluate an expression from its Polish form. An operand stack will be basic to this evaluation algorithm. As operands are encountered in the Polish string they are entered in the stack. Each operator encountered is then applied to the last two operands stacked. In this way the subroutine will reduce an expression to its arithmetic value. In flow chart form the algorithm appears as shown in Fig. 12.21.

To see how the expression subroutine operates, let us trace our expression 70*(X + 100). In parsed form, with the codes stripped, it appears as follows. For tracing purposes we will assume X has value (50).

                70
                X
                100   (X = 50)
                +
                *
                stop

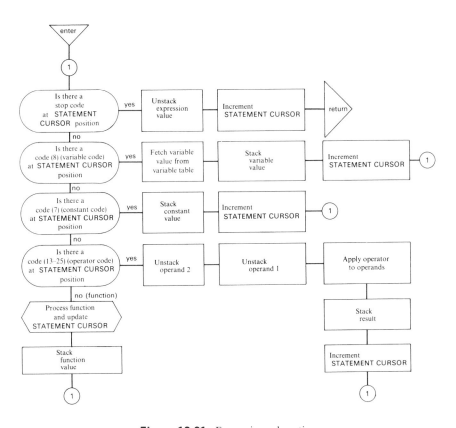

Figure 12.21. Expression subroutine.

On initial entry the stack is empty and **STATEMENT CURSOR** points to 70. The subroutine recognizes 70 as a constant and enters the constant into the stack.

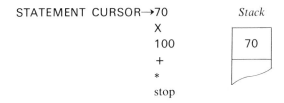

STATEMENT CURSOR→70   *Stack*
              X
             100 | 70 |
              +
              *
             stop

STATEMENT CURSOR is then pushed forward in the Polish string to X. The value of X is taken from the variable table and stacked.

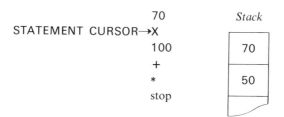

STATEMENT CURSOR is again pushed forward to 100. 100 is recognized as a constant and also stacked.

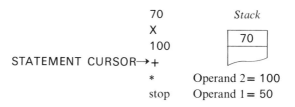

The next item encountered in the Polish string is the "+" operator. It requires that two operands be unstacked.

```
                              70        Stack
                              X        ┌──────┐
                              100      │  70  │
STATEMENT CURSOR→+                     └──────┘
                              *        Operand 2 = 100
                              stop     Operand 1 = 50
```

The "+" operator is applied to the operands (Operand 1 + Operand 2 = 150), and the result is stacked.

```
                              70        Stack
                              100      ┌──────┐
STATEMENT CURSOR→+                     │  70  │
                              *        ├──────┤
                              stop     │ 150  │
                                       └──────┘
```

The subroutine then encounters the operator "∗." Again two operands are unstacked.

70   *Stack*

X

100   (empty)

+

STATEMENT CURSOR→∗   Operand 2 = 150

stop   Operand 1 = 70

The operator is applied to the two operands (Operand 1∗Operand 2 = 10500), and the result is stacked.

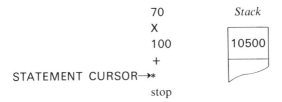

70   *Stack*

X

100   10500

+

STATEMENT CURSOR→∗

stop

Upon encountering the stop code, the expression value is unstacked, and the subroutine excited. The stack is left empty for processing of the next expression.

VALUE= 10500

In the expression subroutine flow chart there is a processing box entitled "Process function and update STATEMENT CURSOR." We must expand on this to show how a function is actually processed.

When a function is encountered, the function parameters are evaluated and passed to the function module. For example, MAX(X + 3,2∗Y) is processed by computing the value of X + 3 and the value of 2∗Y. These values are passed to the function module. There, in the function module, the function value is computed. Function processing could be flow charted roughly as shown in Fig. 12.22.

However, this is not a complete presentation. Actually, function processing can be integrated into the EXPRESSION subroutine. The subroutine will keep an indicator (FUNCTION NEST) that keeps track of and directs function processing. FUNCTION NEST will specify the current level of function nesting within the expression. Examples of function

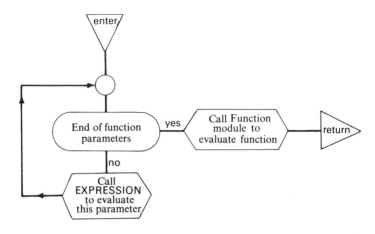

Figure 12.22. Function processing.

nesting levels are as follows.

$$60 + \underbrace{MAX(X - 70, \underbrace{SQRT(72*(Y - 90))}, 50)}$$

FUNCTION NEST   0   1   2   1

The **EXPRESSION** subroutine maintains its internal processing position by keeping track of the current nesting level. This is seen in Fig. 12.23.

For a better understanding, we will write the expression subroutine in compiler-like code. Each statement of the coding will be identified by a statement number. We will then trace a sample expression through the coding, relating the processing to statement numbers. Our expression algorithm appears as follows.

```
(1)   EXPRESSION:   FUNCTION NEST ← 0
(2)   LABEL1:       If position (STATEMENT CURSOR) = stop then do
(3)                 Increment STATEMENT CURSOR
(4)                 If FUNCTION NEST ≠ 0 then go to LABEL2
(5)                 Unstack expression value
(6)                 Return
(7)                 End
```

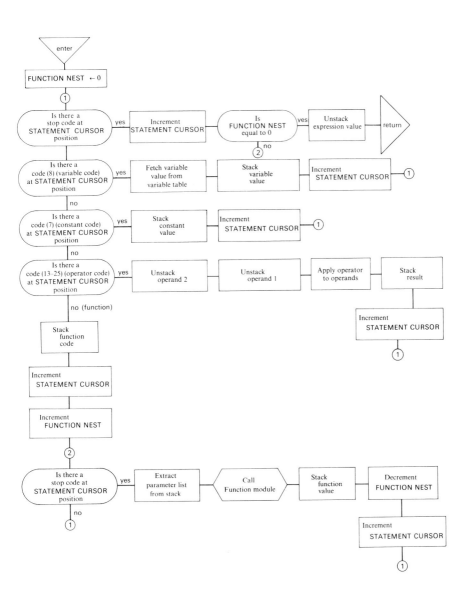

Figure 12.23. Complete expression subroutine.

(8)		If position (STATEMENT CURSOR) = 7 then do
(9)		Stack constant value
(10)		Increment STATEMENT CURSOR
(11)		go to LABEL1
(12)		End
(13)		If position (STATEMENT CURSOR) = 8 then do
(14)		Fetch variable value from variable table
(15)		Stack variable value
(16)		Increment STATEMENT CURSOR
(17)		Go to LABEL1
(18)		End
(19)		If position (STATEMENT CURSOR) = 13 to 25 then do
(20)		Unstack operand 2
(21)		Unstack operand 1
(22)		Apply operator to operands
(23)		Stack result
(24)		Increment STATEMENT CURSOR
(25)		Go to LABEL1
(26)		End
(27)		If position (STATEMENT CURSOR) = 9 to 12 then do
(28)		Stack function code
(29)		Increment STATEMENT CURSOR
(30)		Increment FUNCTION NEST
(31)	LABEL2:	If position (STATEMENT CURSOR) ≠ stop then go to LABEL1
(32)		Extract function list from stack
(33)		Call function module
(34)		Stack function value
(35)		Decrement function nest
(36)		Increment STATEMENT CURSOR
(37)		Go to LABEL1
(38)		End

We have already traced a simple expression, without imbedded functions, through the flow charts. Let us now trace an expression with functions through the compiler code. The expression will be

$$60 + MAX(X - 70, SQRT(72*(Y - 90)))$$

If we assume

$$X = 80$$
$$Y = 92$$

Then

$$Y - 90 = 2$$
$$72*(Y - 90) = 144$$
$$SQRT(72*(Y - 90)) = 12$$
$$X - 70 = 10$$
$$MAX(X - 70, SQRT(72*(Y - 90))) = 12$$
$$60 + MAX(X - 70, SQRT(72*(Y - 90))) = 72$$

We will see these operations carried out as the expression is processed. The expression is processed from its Polish form. As items within the Polish string are processed, a string position is maintained in the STATEMENT CURSOR. The Polish string for our expression, together with its string positions, appears as follows.

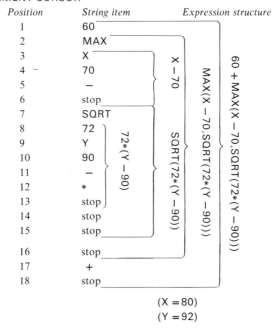

STATEMENT CURSOR

Position	String item
1	60
2	MAX
3	X
4	70
5	−
6	stop
7	SQRT
8	72
9	Y
10	90
11	−
12	*
13	stop
14	stop
15	stop
16	stop
17	+
18	stop

$$(X = 80)$$
$$(Y = 92)$$

Upon entry to EXPRESSION, STATEMENT CURSOR is set to the start of the Polish string (Position = 1). Processing begins in the subroutine by initialization of FUNCTION NEST.

Statement 1   STATEMENT CURSOR is 1
                               FUNCTION NEST ← 0

The first item of the Polish string is recognized as a constant and placed in the operand stack. STATEMENT CURSOR is then updated to the next position.

                               STATEMENT CURSOR is 1
Statements 8-11   Operand stack

                               then STATEMENT CURSOR ← 2

The item at position 2 is recognized as a function code. The parameter list for the function will be built in the operand stack, the first item of the list being the function code.

                               STATEMENT CURSOR is 2
Statements 27-30   Operand stack

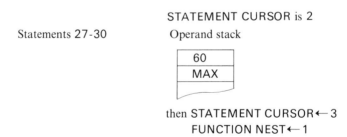

                               then STATEMENT CURSOR ← 3
                               FUNCTION NEST ← 1

Parameters to the MAX function will be evaluated and stacked. The end of function parameter list is designated by a stop code. Therefore, before processing each new parameter, the current function position is tested for the stop code. When the stop code is encountered the parameter list is complete.

At our current processing point for the sample expression, an end of function condition is not detected.

                               STATEMENT CURSOR is 3
Statement 31   (Control is transferred to LABEL1)

At this position, the variable (X) is detected. Its value, 80, is entered in the operand stack.

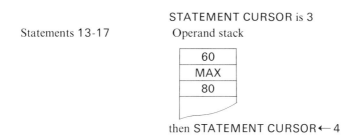

Statements 13-17

STATEMENT CURSOR is 3
Operand stack

| 60 |
| MAX |
| 80 |

then STATEMENT CURSOR ← 4

Similarly the constant, 70, is stacked.

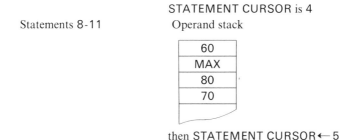

Statements 8-11

STATEMENT CURSOR is 4
Operand stack

| 60 |
| MAX |
| 80 |
| 70 |

then STATEMENT CURSOR ← 5

At position (5) the " − " operator is encountered. Its two operands are unstacked.

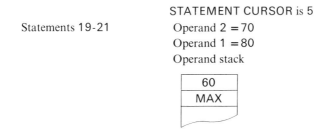

Statements 19-21

STATEMENT CURSOR is 5
Operand 2 = 70
Operand 1 = 80
Operand stack

| 60 |
| MAX |

The operator is applied to its two operands (80 − 70 = 10), and the result is stacked.

	STATEMENT CURSOR is 5
Statements 22-25	Operand stack

60
MAX
10

then STATEMENT CURSOR ← 6

End of function parameter is detected at position (6). Control is passed to LABEL2.

	STATEMENT CURSOR is 6
Statements 2-4	then STATEMENT CURSOR ← 7
	Control is passed to LABEL2

Since there is no stop code in position (7), the parameter list for function (MAX) is not complete. A second parameter to the function must be processed. Control is passed to LABEL1 for this purpose.

	STATEMENT CURSOR is 7
Statement 31	Control is passed to LABEL1

The item at position (7) is recognized as a function. Its code is stacked, and control is passed to LABEL1 for processing the first parameter.

	STATEMENT CURSOR is 7
Statements 27-31	Operand stack

60
MAX
10
SQRT

then STATEMENT CURSOR ← 8
      FUNCTION NEST ← 2
      Control is passed to LABEL1

In position (8) the constant (72) is detected and stacked.

STATEMENT CURSOR is 8

Statements 8-11   Operand stack

| 60 |
| MAX |
| 10 |
| SQRT |
| 72 |

then STATEMENT CURSOR ← 9

The next item encountered is variable (Y). Its value (92) is also stacked.

STATEMENT CURSOR is 9

Statement 13-17   Operand stack

| 60 |
| MAX |
| 10 |
| SQRT |
| 72 |
| 92 |

then STATEMENT CURSOR ← 10

Similarly, the constant (90) is stacked.

STATEMENT CURSOR is 10

Statements 8-11   Operand stack

| 60 |
| MAX |
| 10 |
| SQRT |
| 72 |
| 92 |
| 90 |

then STATEMENT CURSOR ← 11

Upon encountering the " $-$ " operator the last two operands are unstacked.

STATEMENT CURSOR is 11

Statements 19-21   Operand 2 = 90
                       Operand 1 = 92
                       Operand stack

60
MAX
10
SQRT
72

The operator is applied to its two operands $(92 - 90 = 2)$, and the result is stacked.

STATEMENT CURSOR is 11

Statements 22-25   Operand stack

60
MAX
10
SQRT
72
2

then STATEMENT CURSOR ← 12

Similarly, two operands are unstacked for the "*" operator.

STATEMENT CURSOR is 12

Statements 19-21   Operand stack

50
MAX
10
SQRT

The operator is applied ($2*72 = 144$), and the result is stacked.

STATEMENT CURSOR is 12

Statements 22-25   Operand stack

60
MAX
10
SQRT
144

then STATEMENT CURSOR ← 13

End of function parameter is detected by the stop code in position (13).

STATEMENT CURSOR is 13

Statements 2-4   then STATEMENT CURSOR ← 14

Control is passed to LABEL2

The stop code in position (14) signals end of parameter list for the SQRT function. The parameter list is extracted from the operand stack.

STATEMENT CURSOR is 14

Statements 31-32   Operand stack   Function parameter list

60
MAX
10

SQRT
144

The value (12) of the function is computed, and this value is stacked.

STATEMENT CURSOR is 14

Statements 33-37   Operand stack

60
MAX
10
12

then FUNCTION NEST ← 1

STATEMENT CURSOR ← 15

The stop code in position (15) signals the end of the second parameter to MAX. Thereby, control is transferred to LABEL2.

Statements 2-4

STATEMENT CURSOR is 15
then STATEMENT CURSOR← 16
Control is passed to LABEL2

The stop code in position (16) indicates the end of parameter list for MAX. The list is extracted from the operand stack.

Statements 31-32

STATEMENT CURSOR is 16

Operand stack   Function parameter list

| 60 |

| MAX |
| 10 |
| 12 |

The function module is called to evaluate MAX, and the result (12) is stacked.

Statements 33-37

STATEMENT CURSOR is 16
Operand stack

| 60 |
| 12 |

then FUNCTION NEST← 0
STATEMENT CURSOR← 17

Two operands are unstacked for the " + " operator in position (17).

Statements 19-21

STATEMENT CURSOR is 17
Operand 2 = 12
Operand 1 = 60
Operand stack
(empty)

The operator is applied $(60 + 12 = 72)$, and the result is stacked.

STATEMENT CURSOR is 17

Statements 22-25   Operand stack

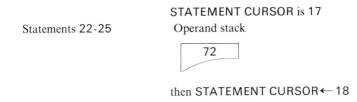

then STATEMENT CURSOR ← 18

The entire expression is terminated by the stop code in position (18). When this is encountered the expression value is unstacked, and the

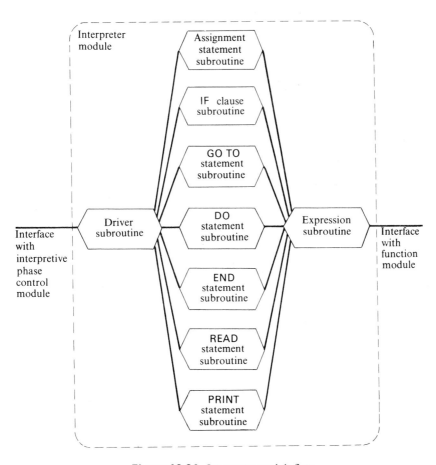

Figure 12.24. Interpreter module flow.

EXPRESSION subroutine is exited.

STATEMENT CURSOR is 18

Statements 2-6   Expression value ← 72

Operand stack

(empty)

then STATEMENT CURSOR ← 19

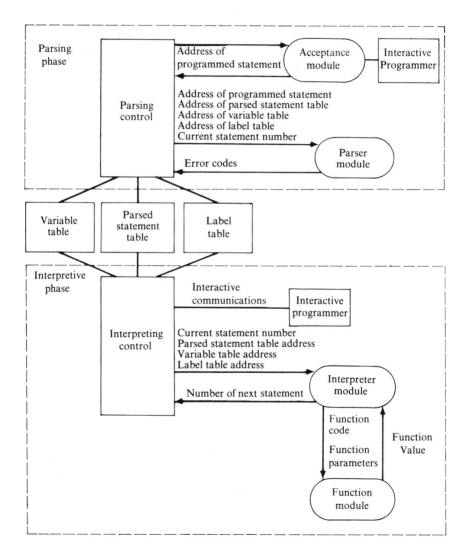

Figure 12.25. System block chart.

This value (72) is, in fact, the proper value for our expression. Note that at the completion of expression processing, STATEMENT CURSOR has been pushed forward past the end of the expression Polish string. The cursor is therefore available for subsequent statement processing elsewhere in the interpreter module.

12.2.7. Interpreter module summary

The expression subroutine we have just traced is but one subroutine of the interpreter module. In all there are nine such subroutines: seven statement subroutines, the expression subroutine, and a driver subroutine. The flow of these nine subroutines is shown schematically in Fig. 12.24, the total flow being the flow of the interpreter module.

12.3. System Summary

The interpreter module is one of six modules comprising our compiler system. In summary, the block chart of all six modules appears as shown in Fig. 12.25.

12.4
exercises

(1) In your own terms define
    (a) the function of the parsing phase
    (b) the function of the interpretive phase.

(2) What is the purpose of the syntax driver?

(3) How does a syntax subroutine interface with the driver?

(4) We have shown separate label and variable tables. How could they be combined in one table?

(5) Consider the method shown for handling DO statements.
    (a) What are the advantages of this method?
    (b) What are the disadvantages?

(6) How is a syntax error position isolated?

(7) What is the breakdown of the interpreter module?

(8) How are functions evaluated in an expression?

13
summary

In the first two sections of the book we discussed techniques and procedures for language processing. These were the tools required to construct a language processing system. In the last section we considered a specific system application. The design and implementation of the system specified which tools, and how they were to be applied, in actual system construction. These basic techniques, together with an overall understanding of how they are used, are what the systems programmer uses in creating a language processing system.

The application language must first be analyzed for structure. We have seen the structure of a simple English sentence schematically illustrated in a tree.

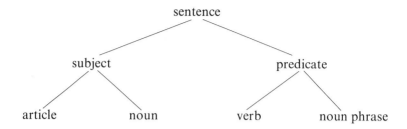

This tree can be reduced to syntax equations.

⟨sentence⟩ :: = ⟨subject⟩ ⟨predicate⟩
⟨subject⟩ :: = ⟨article⟩ ⟨noun⟩
⟨predicate⟩ :: = ⟨verb⟩ ⟨noun phrase⟩

There is a method for using the syntax structure on the computer. The syntax equations are represented internal to the computer in tabular form. A syntax driver then routes statements of the application language through the syntax tables. The statement structure is matched to structures of the syntax tables. If the match is made, the statement is proven to be of legal syntactical structure.

In most applications a statement must be recognized as legal or illegal as well as be broken down and processed. The driven syntax is also of use here. As the statement is scanned for legal form, an internal, coded form of the statement is created. In this form all statement types are classified by unique code numbers. Within the statement, Boolean and arithmetic expressions are carried in Polish form. This enables a fast, efficient statement execution.

For statement execution, an interpretive approach may be chosen. Rather than translating the statement to direct computer language, the statement may be interpreted from its coded form. Tables and lists may be maintained to simulate the programmed transactions; these tables are updated as dictated by the coded transactions.

In a language processing system the table search mechanisms are critical to overall system execution efficiency. The tables are used to hold and resolve programmed symbols. This resolution process requires that symbol tables be searched for matching symbol values. For this, there are several search structures that may be applied. The choice of structures affects the execution efficiency with which the system can resolve a programmed algorithm.

These are the basic elements of language processing. Applied in a direct framework, they are used to create a language processing system. Applied analytically they are used to measure the effectiveness and capability of an existing system. They comprise the techniques and procedures for computer-based linguistic application. It remains the responsibility of the systems programmer and analyst to supply the critical reasoning for effecting their application.

answers to exercises

Chapter 2

(2) In a recursive procedure the calling address and recursion parameters may be tracked upon procedure entry and exit. This order of parameter tracking will always support recursion.

(3) Recursion parameters are tracked in order to preserve the association of a unique set of parameter values to each recursive iteration.

(4) The STACK and UNSTACK mechanisms of Figs. 2.3 and 2.4 may be used.

(5) The parameters may be stacked upon procedure entry and unstacked at exit.

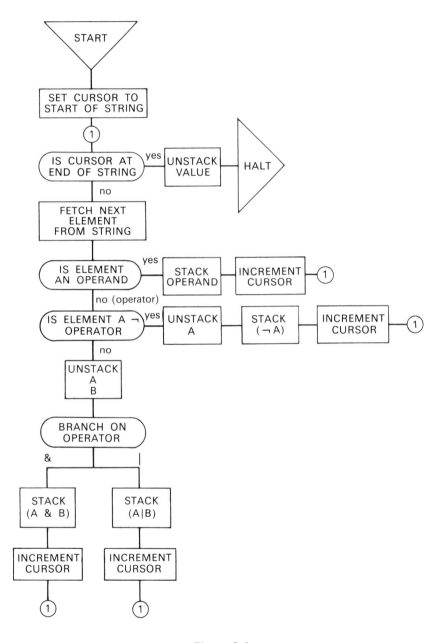

Figure A.1.

Chapter 3

(1) Arithmetic and Boolean expressions may be readily evaluated from their Polish forms by a simple computing procedure.

(2) Operator priorities dictate the order in which operators are evaluated. Higher priority operators are evaluated first.

(3) Operands appear in the same order in the Polish form of an expression as in the standard form.

(4) (a) $37 * 2 +$ (b) $372 + *$
   (c) $327 * +$ (d) AB&C|
   (e) ABC|&   (f) $374 * 2 \uparrow +$

(5) (a) $37 + 64 * -$ (b) $3764 * - +$
           $3764 * - +$ $37 + 64 * -$
   (c) $34 * 2 * 7 -$ (d) $34 * 27 - *$
           $342 * * 7 -$ $3427 - * *$

(6) (a) A ¬   (b) A ¬B|
   (c) AB| ¬   (d) ABC| ¬&

(7) See Fig. 8.1

Chapter 4

(1) Definition of a language by syntax equations declares all legal forms and combinations within that language.

(2) (a) legal   (b) legal
   (c) legal   (d) legal
   (e) illegal   (f) legal
   (g) legal   (h) illegal
   (i) legal

(5) Problems in circular definition and ordering of alternatives may arise when basing a parsing algorithm on syntax equations.

Chapter 5

(1) $\langle$symbol$\rangle ::= \langle$alpha$\rangle \langle$alpha$\rangle \langle$numeric$\rangle \langle$numeric$\rangle \langle$numeric$\rangle$

$$\int_0^5 [\langle alpha \rangle \mid \langle numeric \rangle]$$

$\langle$alpha$\rangle ::= A \mid B \mid C \ldots X \mid Y \mid Z$
$\langle$numeric$\rangle ::= 1 \mid 2 \mid 3 \ldots 8 \mid 9 \mid 0$

(2) ⟨expression⟩ :: = ⟨operand⟩ ∫ [AND ⟨operand⟩ output(AND) |
    OR ⟨operand⟩ output(OR)]
 ⟨operand⟩ :: = ⟨constant⟩ | ⟨symbol⟩ | ⟨subexpression⟩
 ⟨subexpression⟩ :: = (⟨expression⟩)
 ⟨constant⟩ :: = ...
 ⟨symbol⟩ :: = ...

(3)

```
                    CALL EXPRESSION
                    IF INDICATOR ="FALSE" THEN HALT(IMPROPER
                        INFIX STRING)
                    HALT(POLISH TRANSFORMATION COMPLETE)
EXPRESSION:         CALL OPERAND
                    IF INDICATOR ="FALSE" THEN RETURN
EXPRESSION1:        IF NO COMPARE'AND' THEN GO TO EXPRESSION2
                    CALL OPERAND
                    IF INDICATOR ="FALSE" THEN RETURN
                    OUTPUT(AND)
                    GO TO EXPRESSION1
EXPRESSION2:        IF NO COMPARE'OR' THEN INDICATOR ="TRUE",
                        RETURN
                    CALL OPERAND
                    IF INDICATOR ="FALSE" THEN RETURN
                    OUTPUT(OR)
                    GO TO EXPRESSION1
OPERAND:            CALL CONSTANT
                    IF INDICATOR ="TRUE" THEN RETURN
                    CALL SYMBOL
                    IF INDICATOR ="TRUE" THEN RETURN
                    CALL SUBEXPRESSION
                    RETURN
SUBEXPRESSION:      IF NO COMPARE'('THEN INDICATOR ="FALSE",
                        RETURN
                    CALL EXPRESSION
                    IF INDICATOR ="FALSE" THEN RETURN
                    IF NO COMPARE')'THEN INDICATOR ="FALSE",
                        RETURN
                    RETURN:
CONSTANT: ...
SYMBOL: ...
```

(4) ⟨expression⟩ :: = ⟨priority2⟩ ∫ [/ ⟨priority2⟩ output(/) |
    * ⟨priority2⟩ output(*)]

$\langle\text{priority2}\rangle ::= \langle\text{priority1}\rangle \int [\uparrow \langle\text{priority1}\rangle \underline{\text{output}(\uparrow)}]$

$\langle\text{priority1}\rangle ::= \langle\text{operand}\rangle \int [+ \langle\text{operand}\rangle \underline{\text{output}(+)} | $
$\qquad\qquad\qquad - \langle\text{operand}\rangle \underline{\text{output}(-)}]$

$\langle\text{operand}\rangle ::= \langle\text{constant}\rangle | \langle\text{symbol}\rangle | \langle\text{subexpression}\rangle$

$\langle\text{subexpression}\rangle ::= (\langle\text{expression}\rangle)$

(5) $\langle\text{expression}\rangle ::= \langle\text{operand}\rangle \int [\langle\text{operator}\rangle \langle\text{operand}\rangle]$

$\langle\text{operator}\rangle ::= + \underline{\text{output(addition code)}} | / \underline{\text{output(division code)}} | $
$\qquad\qquad \uparrow \underline{\text{output(exponentiation code)}} | - \underline{\text{output(subtraction code)}} | $
$\qquad\qquad * \underline{\text{output(multiplication code)}}$

$\langle\text{operand}\rangle ::= - \underline{\text{output(unary minus)}} \langle\text{operand}\rangle | $
$\qquad\qquad + \underline{\text{output(unary plus)}} \langle\text{operand1}\rangle | \langle\text{operand1}\rangle$

$\langle\text{operand1}\rangle ::= \langle\text{constant}\rangle | \langle\text{symbol}\rangle | \langle\text{subexpression}\rangle$

$\langle\text{subexpression}\rangle ::= (\underline{\text{output(open parenthesis)}} \langle\text{expression}\rangle)$
$\qquad\qquad\qquad \underline{\text{output(close parenthesis)}}$

Chapter 6

(1) Syntax equations are represented by syntax tables.

(2) The syntax driver maintains the following indicators:

SYNTAX POSITION: Current syntax table pointer
INPUT CURSOR: Pointer to input string being parsed
OUTPUT CURSOR: Pointer to output string being created.

(3) A "repeat" structure in a syntax equation can be split off in a separate syntax table.

(4) Syntax subroutines can interface with the syntax driver through the INPUT CURSOR, OUTPUT CURSOR and the TRUE/FALSE return condition.

Chapter 7

(1) Data structures may be kept in list or table form.

(2) The list provides flexibility in arrangement and order while the table affords a quick, simple construction.

(3) An auxiliary stack can be used when data items are of fixed length.

(4) With an auxiliary stack the table need not be compressed after item deletion.

(5) Each data structure can be kept as a list; the list items chained into a common buffer area.

(6) A tree could be structured such that all nodes chained to a node(X) are sons of X.

For example

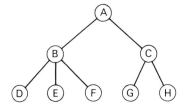

In the above tree B is son(A), H is son(C) and B is father(D).

The uncle and nephew relationships can then be given in terms of father and son.

uncle(X) = other sons(father(father(X)))

nephew(X) = sons(other sons(father(X)))

Chapter 8

(1) The efficiency of a search structure is measured by the speed of the supported search, insert and deletion mechanisms. A machine independent measure of this speed is the number of data items accessed during a search, insert and deletion.

(2)

		Search	Insert	Deletion
(a)	Linear search	50	1	50
	Binary search	≈ 6	≈ 56	≈ 56
	Balanced tree search	≈ 6	≈ 12	≈ 30
(b)	Linear search	500	1	500
	Binary search	≈ 10	≈ 510	≈ 510
	Balanced tree search	≈ 10	≈ 16	≈ 34
(c)	Linear search	5000	1	5000
	Binary search	≈ 13	≈ 5013	≈ 5013
	Balanced tree search	≈ 13	≈ 19	≈ 37

(3) (a)

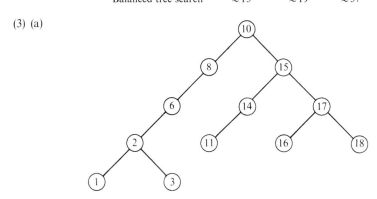

(b)

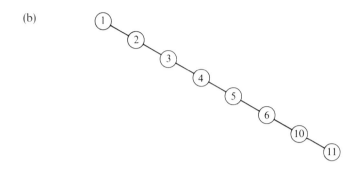

(4)

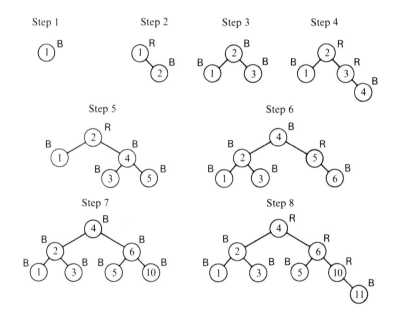

(5) Balance algorithm steps are applied as follows:

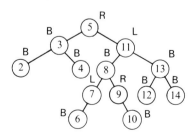

Step 1:   initial adjustment

Step 2:   search for prime position $[X_f = \text{node}(5)]$

Step 3:   call step 4 (root node(11))

Step 4:   auxiliary adjustment

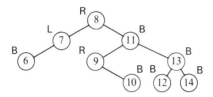

Return to Step 3:   new root-node(8)

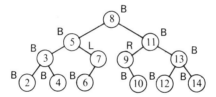

Step 2:   search for prime position [terminate process with $f = 0$]

(6) (a) The hash table could contain 1300 data entries, each entry eight characters in length. Collisions in the hash table could then be resolved through a second collision table.

(b) When data items are of variable length the hash table itself may contain pointers to data items. In this way the hash table can be directly accessed through a hash index : the data item accessed indirectly through that hash table pointer.

(7) (a) Each assembled program contains 200 symbols. At the beginning of an assembly the symbol table is empty ; at completion the table contains 200 entries. Thus, during the assembly process the average number of symbol table entries is 100. The data processing requirements for an assembly can then be approximated as

200 inserts to a 100 item table
1000 searches of a 100 item table

The expected number of data items accessed for the 200 inserts and 1000 searches are as follows :

Linear search structure : $200 * 1 + 1000 * 50 = 50{,}200$

Binary search structure: $200 * 56 + 1000 * 6 = 17{,}200$
Balanced tree search structure: $200 * 12 + 1000 * 6 = 8{,}400$

(b) The algorithm can use a stack table to work through branches and sub-branches of the tree. Working down a branch the nodes encountered will be stacked. The stack table then serves as a trace of the branch when working back up. The algorithm appears as follows:

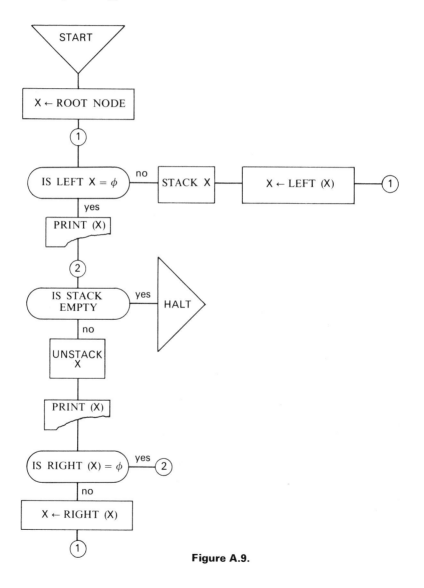

Figure A.9.

(c) The hash structure does not support an alphabetical ordering for concordance listings.

(8) (a) The linear and binary search structures can maintain a symbol table (8 characters per symbol). The tree structure must maintain a doubly linked list (12 characters per symbol). The storage requirements are then as follows:

> Linear search: 8000 characters
> Binary search: 8000 characters
> Tree search: 12,000 characters

(b) Optimum storage requirements would be effected as follows. The linear search structure would keep a variable length table (4 characters of data plus a 1 character length indicator for each item). In the binary search structure a table of data item pointers would be kept together with a length indicator (2 character pointer plus 4 characters of data plus a 1 character length indicator for each item). The tree structure would maintain a doubly linked list plus a length indicator (4 characters for pointers plus 4 characters of data plus a 1 character length indicator). The storage requirements are then as follows:

> Linear search structure: 5000 characters
> Binary search structure: 7000 characters
> Tree search structure: 9000 characters

(c) With fixed length symbols 8 characters per entry would be required in the hash and collision tables. With variable length symbols the hash table would contain pointers to data items (2 character pointer plus 4 characters of data plus a 1 character length indicator); the collision table could be kept as a variable length table (4 characters of data plus a 1 character length indicator for each item). The total data requirements (assuming a 1300 entry hash table and a 200 entry collision table) would then be as follows:

> Fixed length symbols: 12,000 characters
> Variable length symbols: 10,100 characters

Chapter 10

(1) Task segmentation and segment delineation are two basic steps in preparing a design.

(3) Each segment should stand as a logically complete entity.

(4) A programming design can be conveniently summarized in a block chart.

(5) Segments can be allocated as independent work units to separate portions of the programming staff.

(6) Task segmentation provides a framework for selecting programming techniques.

(7) A modular system is broken into distinct independent segments.

Chapter 11

(1) Two goals in designing a language processing system are the segmentation of the system into distinct modules and the definition of each module.

(2) A direct or interpretive processing philosophy may be used in a language processing system.

(3) The direct approach provides more efficient operation. The interpretive approach is more readily adapted to an interactive environment.

(4) The compiler is broken into a parsing and interpretive phase.

(5) Entries in the label table contain a label name together with the associated statement number. Variable table items carry the variable name together with a value entry.

(6) The system block chart should declare the system modules together with the inputs to and outputs from each module.

(7) The coded form is convenient for statement execution.

Chapter 12

(2) The syntax driver directs the parsing of the incoming language.

(3) Syntax subroutines may interface with the syntax driver through the following:

> INPUT CURSOR
> OUTPUT CURSOR
> TRUE/FALSE return conditions

(4) Label and variable entries could be combined in one table by one of two methods.
  (a) Maintain a label/variable flag for each entry
  (b) Restrict the use of variable names for label names.

(5) The method shown for handling DO statements is quick and simple. The real disadvantage to the method is that it does not support GO TO statements which transfer control out of a DO range.

(6) The syntax driver keeps track of the furthest position reached by the INPUT CURSOR. If a statement is shown in error then this position is the error position.

(7) The interpreter module is broken into nine subroutines: one subroutine for each statement type, a driver subroutine and a common expression subroutine.

(8) A function is evaluated by first evaluating each expression used as a function argument. The function value is then computed from its argument values.

index